D0507166

"*The Candlemaker's Companion* is very nicely laid out, organized, and easy to follow. If you want to start a candlemaking library, it is a must-have."

Richard Hansen, President
Bitter Creek Candle Supply, Inc.

"After being in this business for 29 years, I still refer to *The Candlemaker's Companion.* It is the most comprehensive publication written in the last 25 years. I also refer new and experienced candlemakers to the book for problem solving and general information."

Bob Irving
Dussek Campbell, Inc.

"I have told so many candlemakers about this book! It is an exceptional tool."

Michelle Waye, owner
Candle Equipment and Sales, Inc.

"A few years back, I was interested in learning the art of hand dipping candles as a hobby and started scouting out information any place I could find it — bookstores, libraries, and the internet. There was a fair amount of resource material, but *The Candlemaker's Companion* became my primary tutorial because it was written by an impassioned candlemaker and contained an interesting mix of technical, practical, and creative information. I devoured the entire book, confident that I was ready for my first dip, a yield of just 25 pairs. The first candles were wonderfully primitive and were received with great enthusiasm from friends and family. I was hooked.

   With my partner, Gary Briggs, I've since created and grown a small cottage business that sells hand-dipped tapers to more than 1,500 stores across the United States. I'm certainly Betty Oppenheimer's greatest fan, and you can be sure that every dipper we hire has mandatory reading of *The Candlemaker's Companion.*"

Brian Schnetzer, founder
Aunt Sadie's Candlestix

THE
CANDLEMAKER'S
COMPANION

A COMPLETE GUIDE TO ROLLING, POURING, DIPPING, AND DECORATING YOUR OWN CANDLES

BETTY OPPENHEIMER

Storey Publishing

The mission of Storey Publishing is to serve our customers by publishing practical information that encourages personal independence in harmony with the environment.

Edited by Sonja Hakala and Karen Levy
Cover design by Susan Bernier and Meredith Maker
Cover and interior illustrations by Laura Tedeschi
Text design and production by Susan Bernier
Production assistance by Deborah Daly
Based on an original design by Carol Jessop, Black Trout Design
Indexed by Word•a•bil•ity
Technical assistance from Daniel Junkins
The author thanks Pourette, Barker Candle Supplies, and Dussek-Campbell Wax for their help in providing materials and equipment for candle testing.

The information in this book is true and complete to the best of our knowledge. All recommendations are made without guarantee on the part of the author or Storey Publishing. The author and publisher disclaim any liability in connection with the use of this information. For additional information please contact Storey Publishing, 210 MASS MoCA Way, North Adams, MA 01247.

Storey books are available for special premium and promotional uses and for customized editions. For further information, please call 1-800-793-9396.

The Candlemaker's Companion was first published in 1997. All of the information in the previous edition has been reviewed and revised so that this version represents the most up-to-date information available on the topic of candlemaking.

Printed in the United States by R.R. Donnelley

10 9 8 7 6 5

Library of Congress Cataloging-in-Publication Data

Oppenheimer, Betty, 1957–
    The candlemaker's companion: a complete guide to rolling, pouring, dipping, and deco-
    rating our own candles / by Betty Oppenheimer.— Rev. ed.
        p. cm.
    ISBN-13: 978-1-58017-366-7 (alk. paper)
    1. Candlemaking.   I. Title.
TT896.5.067 2001
745.593'32—dc21   00-053802

Contents

ACKNOWLEDGMENTS

To Joshua Sage and Janette Force of Coyote Found Candles, who had the faith to hire me, immersed me in candle manufacturing, believed in my ideas, and put up with my idiosyncrasies.

To my husband, Irv Mortensen, whose gentle soul and support keep me steady.

To my parents, Elaine, Bert, and Lee, who let me play in messy arts and crafts materials, and who taught me personal accountability and the value of learning as a lifelong process.

To Grandma Kate and Aunt Bert, who practiced the needle and cooking arts every day of their lives, and shared them with me.

To Ottar Larsen and Allan Arnold, who helped me find myself when I was lost.

I thank you all for being a part of my growth, my capabilities, and my life. This book is dedicated not only to those who do crafts, but also to those whose support allows our crafts to flourish.

"When you have a taste for exceptional people, you always end up meeting them everywhere."

—Pierre MacOrlan

A Plea from the Author

▼▼▼▼▼

Please, please, please, burn candles! Too many people save them, look at them, fondle them, keep them wrapped up in a drawer or forever in the same centerpiece holder, never to be burned.

It breaks my heart. Candles look their best when they're burning. The glow of a beautiful candle, different with every combination of wax and wick, is the source of candlemaking's romance, ritual, and pride. I urge you to kindle your candles and your heart.

On a practical level, you will need to burn your candles to test the compatibility of your wax and wick. The more you burn, the less painful it will be to see your work go up in flames, and the more you will appreciate the fruits of your labor. And from a craftsperson's point of view, you will want your friends and family to use the gifts you offer.

If they're burning them, they'll want more. In the industry, we call this "repeat business." Lead by example, and burn your work!

> *My candle burns at both ends:*
> *It will not last the night;*
> *But, ah, my foes, and, oh, my friends —*
> *It gives a lovely light!*
>
> —Edna St. Vincent Millay, "First Fig"

INTRODUCTION

The ways we humans use the materials available to us on this planet and how we make things work fascinate me. I've done arts and crafts all of my life; they're my joy, my relaxation, my grounding. I've crossed the line between art and science in various fields that are loosely called "the practical arts." My interest has taken me into fabric laboratories, goose down–processing plants, intaglio printing studios, kitchens, industrial laundries, and my own backyard garden. I'm a practical person who loves to make beautiful things and I'm blessed with a sense of color and design, an analytical mind, and a healthy curiosity.

Crafts provide me with an opportunity to fill my cup of wonder and to make things by hand. There is a special feeling of accomplishment when I use handmade products. There's an earthiness about them, a sense of being a part of the ecology of the earth, of not wasting what has been given. Doing arts and crafts continuously renews my bond with the earth and nature. As a part of nature, and as a steward of the earth, I can take from the earth and fully utilize various foods and fibers, then return their seed to produce more. The natural arts allow me to create without polluting, to compost my mistakes, to grow new materials, and to feel tremendously grounded and centered in the process.

There is a sense of wonder to it all — how did people discover all these amazing foods, fibers, recipes, and chemical reactions we take for granted today? From controlled fire, to yeast for leavened bread, to the waxy coating on bayberries that burns in candles to provide light, we owe our lives and our comfort to these incredible discoveries, yet we rarely stop to notice them. The practical arts are simultaneously a scientific and creative pursuit — they represent the collective wisdom of our species. The spiritual aspect of these skills strikes me in imagined scenes of people performing these very same tasks throughout history. I find myself drifting off in thought while I stir a pot or weed a garden bed — what would it be like to do this if my life depended on it? What would I have been wearing, and how difficult would the lack of tools or different societal customs have made the task, compared with my modern-day re-creation of it? It's the history — the spirit and the connection to all humans throughout time — that makes these arts so wonderful.

I have spent most of my free moments learning and practicing these crafts and my life is fuller for them, and I hope that, if enough of us participate in saving these wonderful, useful skills, we will never have to refer to them as "lost arts." So now that you understand a bit of how and why I love arts and crafts, let's move forward. This is, after all, a book about candlemaking.

My History with Candles

Besides fooling around with some milk-carton candles as a child, I never crafted candles until 1993 when my husband and I decided to "downsize" our lives and move to a small town on the Olympic Peninsula in Washington State. I had spent my prior career years in the textile and garment industry, in New York and later in Seattle, working in production and quality control. I applied for a job at a small candle-manufacturing company called Coyote Found Candles, and was hired as a candle dipper. It was a piece-rate job. I was paid for only what I produced each day, so I learned to do it fast and within Coyote's quality standards.

Being naturally curious, particularly where crafts are concerned, I found myself nosing around the factory and began to want more involvement. Eventually, I was offered a job as production manager and supervised a production staff of nine to eighteen people, making and packaging dipped candles and a variety of other wax- and candle-related products. I designed new candles, formulated colors, and did research and development on new products.

Coyote offered me an opportunity to learn another of the practical arts, and to see how consumers responded to a high-quality, handmade product. It is true that candles can be mass-produced and sold at a lower price, but people do recognize quality, and there is no question that a handmade candle is a thing of beauty and a joy to burn.

In ten years, Coyote Found Candles grew from one man in his chicken coop with an idea, a burner, and a can of wax to over one million dollars in gross sales! While this book is not about how to succeed in business as a candlemaker, it is clear to me that by using the methods presented in this book, you can make candles that are every bit as beautiful as those you buy.

People have been making their own candles, torches, and lamps for thousands of years. At this point, technological advances make the process easier than it has ever been. Once you've mastered the basic techniques of candlemaking, you'll be limited only by time, materials, and your own imagination. This book will cover:

◆ the practical: the basic "how-to" for a particular technique
◆ the technical: answering the question "Why does this work?"
◆ the creative: inventing unique candles of your own design

The actual techniques of making candles are relatively easy. It is the various combinations of waxes, wicks, and methods that make this craft complex. Throughout the book, I will offer advice based on my experience, but much of your success will rest on trial and error and the materials you choose. The differences among materials and the impact these differences may have on your finished product are the challenge of candlemaking.

As you make candles, I strongly urge you to keep a notebook of the materials, temperatures, and techniques you use for each batch of candles so that if your candles are not quite what you had in mind, your notes will help you to figure out where the problems may have originated. Changing one component at a time will often help you figure out how to improve the product. At the least, your notes will help you remember what you did so you can repeat your successes. In looking at and burning the finished product, you can determine and track what needs to be changed.

One of the great things about candlemaking is that all of the wax can be remelted and reused, so no project is ever a total disaster. Materials can be mixed, colored, diluted, made into candles, burned for a while, and remelted for new projects.

As you proceed with your candlemaking, you'll encounter conflicting information regarding the "proper" use of materials from suppliers,

particularly as to wax additives and wick sizes. While my research with candles enables me to offer the guidelines and recipes contained within these pages, I encourage individual innovation and use of regionally available materials.

This book is by no means an end. It is offered as a jumping-off point for the would-be candlemaker. Whether you choose to maintain historical accuracy or strive for optimum use of the most modern wax additives, the techniques outlined here will help you get started and further your adventures in candlemaking. Should this book spark your interest, I urge you to do further reading, and request, from the suppliers listed on page 183, as much information as you can get. Though available information may appear to be contradictory, in reality it offers opportunities to test and improve your own product!

Few people learn every technique thoroughly; most find their personal preferences and proceed to hone their skill in a specific technique, rather than remain partially skilled in many. Once you find your personal passion, explore it. There is a wealth of information available on candlemaking in libraries, museums, craft stores, magazines, and even in children's books.

Now let's proceed with my treatise on the practical art of candlemaking. May you find joy, relaxation, and grounding in the practice of this craft.

". . . joy delights in joy."

— William Shakespeare, "Sonnet 8"

CANDLE NOTES

Keeping notes of what you do in candlemaking is very valuable and will save you lots of time in the long run. It's not just a matter of remembering what you did; your candlemaking notebook is an ongoing history of what worked and what didn't. My candle notes include:

◆ What type of wax and wick did I use? Later, when I'm burning my candles, I can go back to the notes and add comments on the good or bad results.

◆ How much wax, stearic acid, and other additives did I melt, and how much material was left over when I was done? By subtracting one from the other, I learn how much material was used in the project.

◆ At what temperature was the wax when I made the candle?

◆ Did I mix different types of wax? What did I use and in what quantities? What were the results?

◆ What colors did I blend, in what proportions to achieve what color? As in all arts and crafts, knowing how you made a color the first time will let you reproduce it a second time.

◆ How much and what kind of scenting agent did I use?

◆ If my candle is molded, I note how long it took to cool and its diameter. If you want to make several candles in one day and have only one mold, knowing this whole start-to-finish time is important.

◆ Where did I purchase the materials I used? I keep notes on where I buy my wicks, wax, additives, colors, scents, holders, equipment, molds, moldmaking materials, and anything else I use in candlemaking. If I order something from a supplier, I note the name of the person who took my order. As you get into more sophisticated waxes and moldmaking materials, you'll probably need technical assistance from time to time and it helps if you've developed a relationship with an individual at your supplier.

My general rule about candle notes is to write down everything I would need to know if I wanted to explain what I've done to someone else in a few weeks. What would that person want or need to know?

CHAPTER 1
The History and Language of Candles

Humans have used light to lengthen and lighten their days for 15,000 years. Hollowed-out stones filled with animal fat and used as lamps were among the earliest light sources. Modern-day oil lamps work in much the same way, with a wick pulling fuel up to a flame. Early methods of torch lighting involved soaking papyrus, flax, or other fibers in resins, pitch, or natural oils and burning them as torches. This technique progressed to the use of twisted fibers dipped in various combustible substances that remain solid at room temperature. These dipped fibers were early versions of candles.

WHAT IS A CANDLE?

A candle is a body of tallow, wax, or other fatty material formed around a wick composed of braided cotton threads and used for a portable light. In other words, a candle is a solid chunk of fuel wrapped around a wick. A candle works because the wick burns and melts the solid fuel into a liquid, which is transported by capillary action ("wicked") to the flame, which vaporizes the fuel and burns it off.

A Brief History of Candles

It is hard to imagine the world of early candlelight, with its wide variety of materials, the hundreds of years with few or no technological breakthroughs, and the fact that the match (that little item we take for granted every day) was not invented until 1827!

Early candles were made of vegetable waxes produced from plants such as bayberries, candelilla leaves, candletree bark, esparto grass, and various varieties of palm leaves such as carnauba and ouricury. They were also made of animal tissue and secretions, such as spermaceti (whale oil), ambergris, and beeswax (insect secretions). Sometimes,

Lamps and Candles

If a fuel remains liquid at room temperature, like oil, the result is a lamp. If a fuel is solid at room temperature, like wax, the result is a candle.

Liquid fuel is burned in a lamp.

Shine On

The word "candle" comes from the Latin, *candela*, "a light or torch," and from *candere*, "to shine or be bright."

entire animals such as the stormy petrel and the candlefish of the Pacific Northwest were threaded with a wick and burned as candles. Tallow candles were made of sheep, cow, or pig fat. All these candles were rather crude, time-consuming to make, and smoky.

Of the two kinds of candle fuel, beeswax was considered the better product as it burned cleaner than tallow and had a lovely odor compared to tallow's rancid, smoky burn. Being scarce, beeswax was much more expensive. Only churches and the wealthy could afford beeswax candles. In fact, church rules insisted on beeswax candles because of the belief that bees were blessed by the Almighty. It was ordered that mass be performed by the light of wax made by bees, even during the day, as they represented spiritual joy.

Early chandlers dipped wicks into melted wax or poured wax over wicks repeatedly until a thick coating built up. In the fifteenth century wooden molds were developed, but they could not be used for beeswax because it was too sticky to release from wooden surfaces. The molded

DONATIONS

In the Middle Ages, church donations could be made in the form of wax, known as wax-shot or wax-scot. Wax was considered to represent the flesh of Jesus Christ, the wick was his soul, and the flame was the Divinity, which absorbs and dominates the flesh and soul.

The oily candlefish was used as a torch.

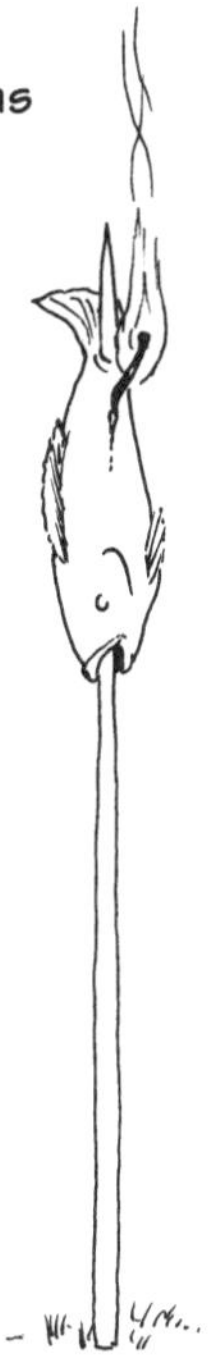

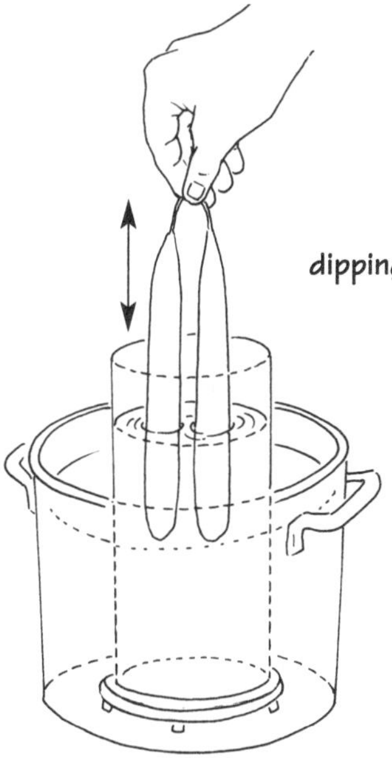

dipping candles

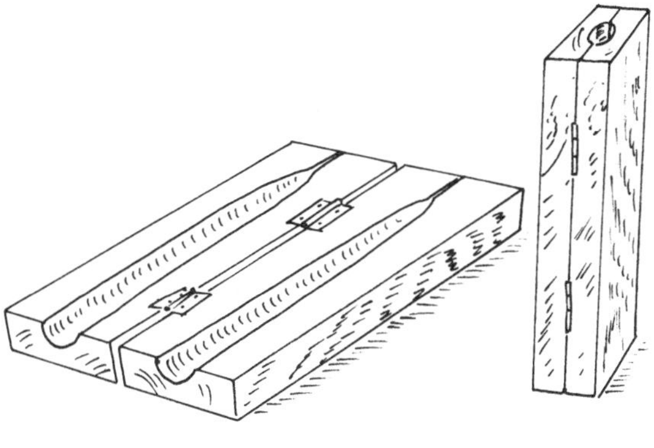

hinged candle mold

candlemaking method did make the process of forming tallow candles much easier, however, and tallow candles became more available and affordable. Still, candles burned quickly and their wicks had to be continuously trimmed (originally called snuffing) to prevent smoking.

By the seventeenth century, European state edicts controlled the weight, size, and cost of candles. In 1709, an act of the English Parliament banned the making of candles at home unless a license was purchased and a tax paid. Rushlights, made by dipping rushes or reeds in suet, were excluded from the tax and became the cheapest form of lighting. But, surprisingly, many peasants still bought the more expensive candles because their impoverishment meant less meat — and less suet —in their diet.

The nineteenth century finally brought with it a burst of new discoveries and inventions that revolutionized the candle industry and made lighting available to all. In the early- to mid-nineteenth century, a process was developed to refine tallow with alkali and sulfuric acid. The result was a product called stearin. Stearin is harder and burns longer than unrefined tallows. This breakthrough meant tallow candles could be made without the usual smoke and rancid odor. Stearins were also derived from palm oils, so vegetable waxes as well as animal fats could be used to make candles.

Also in the nineteenth century, a method was developed for braiding wick fibers. This caused them to bend over and away from a candle's flame, where they would burn to ash and eliminate the need for the constant snuffing, or trimming, of a candle's wick. In addition, chemical treatments were developed for wick fibers that made them less flammable, so candles would burn longer and more efficiently.

Matches, which were invented in 1827 using poisonous phosphorus, improved by the end of the century, eliminating the need for sparking with flint, steel, and tinder, or for keeping a fire burning 24 hours a day.

But probably most important of all, paraffin was refined from oil around 1850, making petroleum-based candles possible. The combination of paraffin, which burns cleanly and without odor, and stearins, which harden soft paraffin, with new wick technologies developed in the nineteenth century, revolutionized the candle industry, giving us the tools and materials we still use for candle manufacturing.

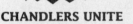

CHANDLERS UNITE

Formal candlemakers' guilds were in place by the thirteenth century, and the candlemakers in them were separated into tallow chandlers (those who made candles from animal fats) and wax chandlers (those who made candles from beeswax). In fact, the Paris tax rolls of 1292 listed some 71 chandlers.

While candlemaking materials improved, however, kerosene became popular as a less expensive and readily available replacement for whale oil lamp fuel. When this happened, oil lamps became the preferred source of artificial light. So even though candles improved in the nineteenth century, they never held as important a position as they did when they were the only available light source. In fact, twentieth-century sales in candles are on a par with late-nineteenth-century sales.

Nowadays, candles are used predominantly for romantic atmosphere, during electrical outages, and in spiritual quests and religious rituals. We share this with our nineteenth-century relatives — we never stopped using candles, even after we no longer needed them!

DO YOU SPEAK "CANDLE"?

In order for us to communicate clearly throughout this book, you need to know a few candle terms. Candles are named for their shape or by the method used to make them.

Candle Shapes

Container. Any candle that is poured into a container and intended to be burned in the container is a container candle. These candles are often made of soft wax and would not be able to stand on their own outside their enclosures.

The container also prevents soft wax from dripping. Since these candles are safely contained in a vessel, they are often used in restaurants and in religious rituals that require long-burning candles.

Pillar. A thick candle with a geometrical cross section such as a circle, oval, or hexagon is called a pillar. It is usually referred to by its diameter followed by its height. For example, a 3- by 6-inch pillar would be 3 inches in diameter and 6 inches high. Some pillars come in standard sizes for commercial and religious use but you can make many variations of pillars by using molds.

Novelty. These are irregularly shaped candles made by molding, sculpting, and/or pouring.

"I shall light a candle of understanding in thine heart, which shall not be put out."

—The Apocrypha, II Esdras 14:25

Candles are identified by their shapes.

Votive Time

Votives are generally referred to by the length of time they burn in their containers. The 10-hour and the 15-hour votives are the most popular.

Taper. These are the long cylindrical candles that kindle memories of historic candle-dipping. Tapers can be made by dipping wicks into melted wax, by pouring wax into a mold, and by rolling wax around a wick. No matter the method, the result is always candles made to fit into a holder.

Tapers are generally made ½ inch or ⅞ inch in diameter at the base because most holders are designed to fit these two sizes. There are, of course, exceptions, such as birthday candles (³⁄₁₆ inch) and Danish tapers (¼ inch). Some specialty candleholders are designed to hold a taper larger than ⅞ inch.

Votives and Tea Lights. Although these candles originated in the church, the term now refers to small plug-type candles that are 1½ inches in diameter by 2 to 3 inches high. This shape has become popular for scented candles because their small size allows them to fit easily in small rooms, such as bathrooms.

As votives melt and become liquid in their containers, the wick uses up all the liquid fuel. If you burn a votive on a plate, the burn time will be shorter because the wax will drip and the wick will be unable to use it.

Tea lights are small votives used to warm pots of potpourri and to heat foods. They fit in smaller-than-standard votive cups.

Methods of Making Candles

Cast and Molded. These candles are made by pouring wax into a preformed mold or shape. Molds can be made of disposable materials such as milk cartons and sand, purchased in metal or plastic, found at garage sales and on the beach, or created by you out of rubber, latex, or silicone rubber. You can make any of the candle shapes listed in the previous section with the molding and casting method.

Dipped. These candles are made by repeatedly dipping a piece of wick into melted wax in a container, or dipping can. The results are called tapers because this is the natural shape that occurs as a result of dipping.

Drawn. This is an old method made new by modern technology. It involves pulling long lengths of wick (thousands of yards) through melted wax. This method works well for making small-diameter candles such as birthday candles, or the long waxed wicks used to light multiple candles called wax matches. In earlier times, some lamps were designed to hold wound lengths of waxed wick, which were unwound as they burned down. This method allowed a long-burning candle without a thick wax product.

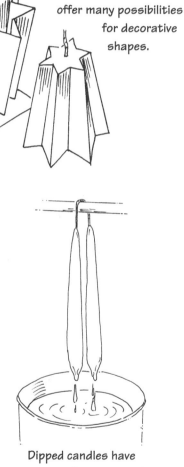

Metal candle molds offer many possibilities for decorative shapes.

Dipped candles have a natural taper.

Wick is drawn through wax to create long-burning candles.

Extruded. This is a machine method that pushes wax out through a shaped template, much like making cookies with a cookie gun. Once they're extruded, these very long candles are then sliced into their proper lengths. This method requires accurate heating and cooling of the wax in order to ensure that the intended shape holds as the wax comes through the die.

Poured. This term refers to an old-fashioned method of pouring wax repeatedly over a wick to build it up to candle size.

Pressed. This is a newer method of making commercial candles in which wax is atomized onto a cooling drum, forming wax beads or granules. These beads are then compressed into molds, where they bind to form a candle. The commercial advantage of pressed candles is that they can be removed from molds much more quickly than molten-poured molded candles.

Rolled. These candles are made by rolling sheets of wax around a wick. Tapers, pillars, and novelty candles can be made with this method.

Now that you've learned some history and candle language, let's get to the craft of making candles.

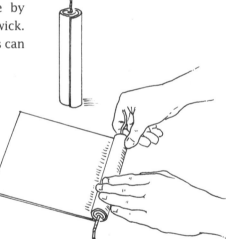

Wax is rolled around a wick to create tapers, pillars, and novelty candles.

CHAPTER 2
Wick

A wick is a braided (plaited) bundle of cotton threads, or plies, that has been mordanted, or pickled in a chemical solution. The wick is perhaps the most important part of the candle. Its relationship to the wax, in terms of burn rate, is what determines whether a candle will burn well or at all.

WHAT MAKES IT BURN?

Prior to the invention of braided, mordanted wick, a variety of twisted fibers were used to carry the flame of a candle. Since they did not curl predictably — modern wicks bend over an exact 90 degrees — the wick stayed in the hottest part of the combustion zone and smoked as it carbonized.

People burning candles prior to the various innovations of the nineteenth century had to "snuff" them frequently. Snuffing means snipping off the wick to ½ inch, to prevent smoking.

Braiding plays an important role in the burning characteristics of a wick. The spaces between the braided plies allow more air into the combustion zone than a nonbraided cord would provide. In addition, braiding forces the wick to bend over as it burns, which means the tip of the wick moves out of the combustion zone and into the oxidizing zone, where it can burn off completely.

The mordanting, or pickling, used on a wick is essentially a fire-retardant solution. It sounds strange to say a candle wick is treated to retard burning, but a candle's wax (fuel) should burn before the wick does so the wick can act as a fuel delivery system between the wax and the flame. The mordant causes the wick to burn more slowly and to decompose fully when it is exhausted.

flat-braided wick

Before lighting a candle, trim the wick to within ¼ inch of the wax surface. This cuts down on the excess carbon that builds up on the wick and prevents the candle's flame from becoming too big.

When burning larger candles, those 3 inches or more in diameter, allow the wax to melt close to the outer edge of the candle before you extinguish it. This will take approximately 2 hours or more, but this melting lets the candle use up the liquid wax, or fuel, evenly and extends the life of the candle.

It's also recommended that candles, especially large-diameter candles, not be burned more than 3 hours at one time. A longer burning time begins to change the structure of the wax and causes difficulties in burning. If you extinguish the candle after 3 hours and let it cool, the wax's structure can reform and ensure an even burn.

Good Combustion

When you're burning your candles, watch the wick and flame in order to determine whether you have achieved good combustion. A candle that is burning well will have a 1- to 2-inch, steadily burning flame (not flickering or sputtering). The wick should be bent over at approximately 90 degrees or sticking straight up and into the oxidation zone at the top

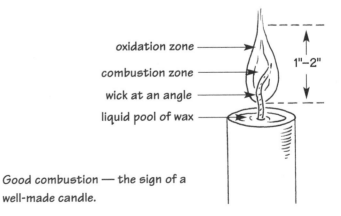

oxidation zone

combustion zone

wick at an angle

liquid pool of wax

1"–2"

Good combustion — the sign of a
well-made candle.

BURN RATE

Burn rate is often used to find out how well a wick and wax combination is performing. Sometimes, by changing the wax mixture and the wick, you can make a candle that will burn significantly longer and is therefore a better value.

To determine burn rate, weigh the candle. Burn it for a measured length of time, extinguish the flame, and reweigh it, including any wax that dripped. The dripped wax is considered unburned since it was not used as fuel by the flame.

Let's say the candle weighed 340 grams, and you burned it for 1 hour, and reweighed it at 40 grams. This means the candle burned 300 grams in 60 minutes. Each minute of burn time used up 5 grams of wax. (300 divided by 60 is 5.) Your burn rate is 5 grams per minute.

of the flame so that the tip is almost to the edge of the flame and can burn to ash. The wax should form a liquid pool surrounding the wick — not so big as to spill over but not so dry that the wick has no liquid to pull up.

TYPES OF WICK

It is difficult to pinpoint exactly what wick you should use for a candle, but there are general guidelines you can follow. Most commonly available candlemaking supplies will indicate which wick is recommended for the wax and type of candle you are making. For example, a wick package will say, "Use this wick for all 1½-inch-diameter candles." This is a good place to start, but be aware that your choice of wax may have as much impact on the success of a candle as the choice of a wick that's termed appropriate for a particular size candle.

Suppliers of wick material usually classify candles by diameter into extra small (0–1 inch), small (1–2 inches), medium (2–3 inches), large (3–4 inches), and extra large (over 4 inches). Within these size guidelines, certain types of wick work better with certain candle shapes and types of wax.

Wicks come in flat-braided, square-braided, and cored styles, and in a range of sizes. Simplified labeling has been adopted by most suppliers so you will not have to memorize the following information, but I suggest you read this information to familiarize yourself with the differences among the three types.

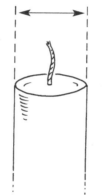

Candle diameter plays an important role in wick selection.

Flat Braid

This is basically what it sounds like — a three-strand braid made of many plies per strand. Flat-braided wick is referred to by the number of plies in the wick, so the larger the number, the larger the wick. Common sizes

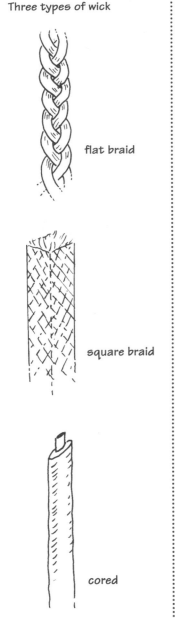

Three types of wick

flat braid

square braid

cored

are 15 ply (extra small), 18 ply (small), 24 and 30 ply (medium), 42 ply (large), and 60 ply (extra large). A major wick producer in the United States says this wick is "for use in rigid dipped self-supporting candles, such as tapers and pillars."

Because these braids are flat and tensioned, the wick bends over when burned and may burn slightly off center, in the side oxidation zone of a flame.

Square Braid

These wicks look like round-cornered squares and come in various sizes with various numbering systems. A major wholesale supplier of wick in the United States uses a numbering system ranging from 6/0 (extra small) to 1/0, then beginning with #1 through #10, which is the largest. The wicks with /0 after the number are regular braid, and the ones with the # symbol in front of the number are loosely woven, so they are fluffier and larger in diameter without actually being heavier.

This supplier states that square-braided wicks are "for use in beeswax candles, also pillars, blocks, and novelties." It is my experience that a 1/0 square-braided wick is roughly equivalent to a 30-ply flat braid. Square-braided wicks tend to stand up straighter than a flat braid, burn off in the upper oxidation zone of a flame, and keep a flame centered in its candle.

Cored Wicks

These wicks have a paper, cotton, zinc, or lead core in the center that holds them erect. Those with metal cores burn hotter than their non-metal equivalents. These wicks are recommended for container candles for two reasons: First, they are usually wax-impregnated and attached to a metal tab so they can be put into the bottom of a container, and will stand upright as you pour wax. Second, the core makes the wick stand upright during burning so that it does not drown in the often large pools of liquid wax formed in container candles. They come in sizes and are generally referred to as small, medium, and large.

If you're experimenting with waxes other than beeswax and paraffin or using extremely large containers, you might need more specifics about the many types of wick available. I once counted 112 types of wick in a wholesale catalog, but for normal use the wicks available through your craft supplier will suffice.

As a beginning candlemaker, you will have your best success with wicks by following the instructions in the catalogs or on the packages provided by the supplier. If a wick does not burn well, you can use the troubleshooting guidelines offered in this book or go back to your supplier and describe what has occurred. In my experience, suppliers are happy to answer questions.

Lead-Cored Wicks

There has been much discussion of late about the potential impact of burning candles with lead-cored wicks. Historically, lead-cored wick has been used for its rigidity and slow, hot burning properties, which held some advantage for container and pillar candles. However, concerns about lead poisoning over the past several decades put lead-cored wick under scrutiny.

Although the Consumer Product Safety Commission could not pinpoint any health hazard from the use of these wicks, the members of the National Candle Association voluntarily agreed to stop using lead-cored and lead-alloy wicks in 1974. Atkins and Pearce, the largest wick producer in the U.S., continued to manufacture lead-cored wick throughout the 1980s, but they reduced production in 1992 and stopped making lead-cored and lead-alloy wicks entirely in 1998. American candle manufacturers have formulated ways to manufacture container and pillar candles without using lead wicks. The majority of candles produced in the United States are now made with 100 percent cotton wick.

However, lead-cored wick enables candlemakers outside the United States to make inexpensive candles and, unfortunately, consumers in the U.S. have bought them by the scores. With the increase in imported candles during the past 25 years (and candles made by small manufacturers who may not be familiar with the voluntary ban), candles with lead-cored

NEW TYPES OF WICK

Over the past decade, as potential environmental problems with lead-cored wicks prompted candlemakers to abandon these wicks, wick manufacturers developed alternative wick options. The new wicks burn hot and remain rigid, as lead-cored wicks did.

Hemp, a bast fiber (in the same plant family as ramie, linen, and jute) that was historically used for rope, is stiff and offers good rigidity with cellulosic burning properties similar to those of cotton. In addition, a coreless wick made in Germany is tightly braided in such a way that it acts like it has an inner core.

New developments are always underway as wick manufacturers respond to the needs of commercial and home candlemakers. You can learn about new candlemaking materials on the many candle sites on the Internet or by perusing the latest version of your candle supplier's catalog.

wick have found their way back into the world market. Recent studies in the relatively new field of indoor air quality have shown that burning lead-cored-wick candles within a home may produce an elevated level of lead in the air. Both the National Candle Association and the Consumer Products Safety Commission support the complete removal of lead-cored wicks from the U.S. market.

Today, the National Candle Association, Consumer Products Safety Commission (CPSC), and American Society for Testing and Materials are working together to develop standards for wicks that the CPSC and retailers can enforce. As more and more consumers learn about the concerns

IS THIS A LEAD-CORED WICK?

If you're out shopping and you see a candle you'd like to buy, you can determine whether it has a lead-cored wick by using this simple method from the National Candle Association:

Take a regular piece of white paper with you to the store. Rub the paper on the tip of an unburned wick. If the wick leaves a light gray pencil-like mark, it has a lead core. Zinc and tin wicks should not leave any mark on the paper. If the wick contains lead, leave the candle behind. Go home and make your own candles!

A wick with a lead core will leave a light gray mark, similar to a pencil mark.

When you are rubbing the paper on the unburnt wick, zinc or tin wicks should not leave any mark on the paper.

associated with lead-cored wick, they are asking storeowners whether their candles contain lead. Storeowners, in turn, are asking candle manufacturers and wholesalers about the wicks used in their candles and are purchasing fewer lead-cored products. In the process, everyone is becoming better educated about the ingredients in candles, and there is a national push to rid the country of candles made with lead-cored wick.

While lead-cored wick offers rigidity in candles that might otherwise drown a drooping wick and burns hot enough to produce a wide pool of wax in large pillar candles, these burning properties can be achieved without this wick. Candlemakers can use nonlead wick and/or change the wax formula to better balance the fuel consumption of the wick. In other words, lead-cored wick is not a necessary evil, and you can avoid it by conducting research and development to find the right proportions of wick to wax.

If you are making container candles that require a rigid, cored wick, I recommend that you use paper core. If metal is absolutely essential for the burn properties of your wax formulation, zinc-cored wicks are available. Bear in mind that half of the research and development you do when formulating a new candle is determining the correct wick; the other half is the proper wax formula. If you take the time to formulate a well-balanced candle, there is no reason to use lead-cored wick.

ESSENTIAL WICK TECHNIQUES

There are several basic techniques you need to know for preparing and inserting wicks into candles.

Priming

Any time you make a candle, the wick must be saturated with wax to eliminate trapped air. Most of the time, this happens naturally as a part of the candlemaking process. Sometimes, with molded or novelty candles, you will need to prime a wick as a separate operation.

Heat your wax to 160°F. Dip the wick into it for 60 seconds. You will see air bubbles exiting the braid. Hold it in the wax until there are no

Hold the wick in the wax until all of the air bubbles escape.

WICK TABBING

The increased interest in container wax and gel candles has prompted new developments in tabs. High-collar tabs have a longer metal tube in which to insert the wick, which helps keep the wick upright, and can even be used in gel candles when they become liquid. The candle will not and should not be burned below the level of the high collar.

In order to keep the wick and tab standing upright during the pouring stage, manufacturers have introduced round, double-sided sticky pads that you affix to the inside of the container. The wick tab is then stuck directly onto the sticky pad, and it will not move or float as you pour the wax or gel.

more air bubbles. Remove the wick and pull it taut until it is cool. It will then be stiff and ready to use. This stiffness allows you to use it almost the way you would use cored wicks. Primed wicks are stiff enough to push through the hole of a hardened candle or push into the hole of a poured-cast candle after the wax has been poured.

Sometimes the largest available cored wick does not burn hot enough for very large candles. Don't despair! Use regular flat- or square-braided wick that you have primed. Or, in the case of very large candles, you can prime an all-cotton shoelace.

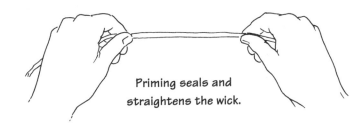

Priming seals and
straightens the wick.

Tabbing

A wick tab is a small square of soft metal with an opening cut in its center. You attach a metal wick tab to a cored wick by inserting the end of the wick into the hole in the tab, then squeezing the metal around the wick with a pair of pliers. The wick is now ready to be inserted into a hardened candle or used in a container into which you will pour wax.

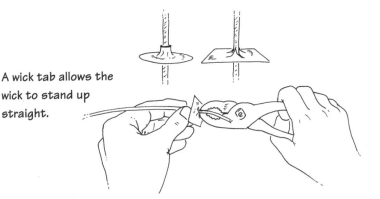

A wick tab allows the
wick to stand up
straight.

Wicking a Hardened Candle

Heat a wicking needle, knitting needle, or ice pick over a candle or other heat source. Push it carefully through the center of a hardened candle until it exits the other end. Thread a cored or primed wick through the hole. You can use a loop of thin wire pushed up through the hole as a needle threader. Pull the wick through the loop and pull the wire back down through the hole. You may fill the hole with wax or allow this filling to happen naturally when the candle is lit. Just remember, if you do not fill the cavity with wax, the wick may slide out of the base of the candle when it is moved around.

Make a wick hole in a hardened candle with a hot ice pick.

MAKING YOUR OWN WICKS

Because I'm the curious type and love needlework, I decided to try making my own wicks. I bought the three sizes of plain cotton crochet yarn available for use in lacemaking and braided them as follows:

- **Speed-CroSheen C-44** is made of 4 plies and each of those plies is a 2-ply. I made a three-strand braid of this yarn. The result is 8 plies of 3 strands to make a 24-ply wick.
- **Knit-Cro-Sheer A-64** is made of 4 single plies in each strand. I used two threads per strand of a three-strand braid. The result is 4 plies of 6 strands to make a 24-ply wick.
- **Three-Cord Crochet B-34** is made of a 3-ply single in each thread. I used six threads per strand of a three-strand braid. The result is 3 plies of 18 strands to make a 54-ply wick.

I also bought various cotton shoelaces to use as wicks because I had read that these "extra-large flat braids" work well in odd-shaped or over-sized candles.

All of the above wicks were mordanted in a solution of 1 part salt, 2 parts sodium borate (borax), and 10 parts water.

When these experimental wicks were soaked for 12 hours and then dried, they became very crystalline and stiff. They burned with a large flame for an hour or so, but then they started to smoke. I went back to the drawing board.

Another book suggested using boric acid rather than sodium borate in the mordanting solution, so I decided to continue my experiment. In order to prevent crystallization, I kept the mordant hot the entire time the wick was soaking.

After the wicks dried, I poured three candles, each with a different test wick — one wick with no mordant, one with mordant made with sodium borate, the third with mordant made of boric acid. All three burned, but all three needed to be snuffed periodically to prevent smoking and to keep the flame at a reasonable size.

Side-by-side burning comparisons
help assess your success.

Because I could not completely control the tension or twist of my braiding, the wicks did not curl properly as they burned, so they were unable to burn to ash in the cooler part of the flame.

None of them burned as well as machine-made wick, but the all-cotton shoelaces worked well in the Citronella Cinderblock candles (see page 86) because these poured candles required a larger-than-commercially-available wick.

Each reference I read lists different chemicals for mordanting, and the process appears to be a closely guarded trade secret. I believe the reason the non-mordanted wick burned as well as the others is that the cotton cord is mercerized (a chemical process using sodium hydroxide for the purpose of shrinking and increasing dyeability of the cotton fiber), so the fiber has already undergone some mordanting.

Upon reflection, I can say that if I needed an extra-large wick or ran out of wick when I was desperate to make candles or had a reason to re-create pioneer life, I would certainly make my own wick. But to make consistent, modern, state-of-the-art candles, I will continue to purchase machine-made wick.

IS THERE A DRAFT IN HERE?

It is important to note that burning candles in a draft will cause dripping, since the oxygen is greater on one side of the candle than on the other. A candle that, in reality, has a perfect ratio of wax to wick, may appear to burn poorly if burned in a draft. Conversely, once a container or large pillar has burned down some, the hole may be so deep that the flame can't receive sufficient oxygen to continue burning. Consider making your container candles with a softer (lower-melting-point) wax so they can maintain a flame in spite of ever-decreasing oxygen levels.

IF YOUR WICK DOESN'T BURN RIGHT

The correct burning of a wick depends largely on the melting point of the wax and the diameter of the candle.

Guttering

Cratering

smoke

carbonized wick

dry wax pool

Carbonized wick

Symptom	Problem
Amount of wax melted by the flame is greater than the wick can absorb and the wax overflows. This is called guttering or dripping.	Wick is too small for type of wax and diameter of candle.
All of the liquid wax runs down the side of the candle, leaving no liquid wax for the wick to absorb, and the candle will smoke until it melts enough wax to burn fuel rather than cotton.	Wick is too small for type of wax and diameter of candle.
The wick may simply burn a craterlike hole down the center of a pillar and drown itself when it gets too deep.	Wick is too small for type of wax and diameter of candle.
Wick smokes, and a bead of carbon forms on the wick.	Wick is too large and absorbs more liquid fuel than can be combusted.
So much of the surrounding wax in a pillar is melting that it drips out before it can be absorbed into the cotton.	Wick is too large.
Candle sputters.	Candle may be poorly made and may have air pockets or water pockets. If this is the case, it will sputter as the wick seeks available fuel. Sometimes these candles are a hopeless loss. Other times they will burn well once the trouble spot has been bypassed.
Wick will not burn.	Wick may be clogged by improper additives or colorings. The most common cause of clogging is the use of pigments. For this reason I do not advocate the use of crayons, lipstick, or paints as colorants.

CHAPTER 3
Wax and Additives

Wax is the fuel that burns in the flame of a candle. Generally speaking, candle wax can be liquefied between 100°F and 200°F and is solid at room temperature. There are waxes from animal, vegetable, and mineral (petroleum) sources. Commercially refined waxes are used in food and pharmaceutical coatings, cosmetics, industrial casting, lubricating, finishing leather and wood, and a host of other applications. Only a few of the commercially available waxes can be used in candlemaking.

TYPES OF WAXES

Nowadays, most candles are made of paraffin or beeswax or some combination of the two. But over the centuries, candlemakers have used a wide variety of waxes. Here's a list of the traditional and modern choices for the candlemaker.

BAYBERRY

This wax is obtained from boiling the berries of the bayberry shrub. The wax naturally floats to the surface and is skimmed off and made into candles. Bayberries were so named because the Pilgrims first found them growing along Cape Cod Bay. But these bushes are found as far north as Nova Scotia, as far south as the Carolinas, and as far west as upstate New York. At present, bayberry wax is very expensive because the berries are not as plentiful as they were in the American colonies. They are known for their sage green color and spicy aroma. Today, most bayberry candles available at a reasonable price are actually paraffin scented with bayberry essential oil. However, some specialty candlemaking-supply houses do offer bayberry wax.

GOOD LUCK IN THE NEW YEAR

A New England tradition, still practiced today, holds that if you receive a bayberry candle as a gift and burn it to the end on New Year's Eve, you will enjoy good luck, good health, lots of friends, and lots of money in the coming year. A saying goes with the tradition: "A bayberry candle burned to the socket puts luck in the home, food in the larder, and gold in the pocket."

If you wanted to create bayberry candles today, you would need 10 to 15 pounds of berries to make a pound of wax, enough for three to five pairs of dipped tapers. The berries would have to be boiled, the impurities filtered out, and the wax used for either dipping or pouring into molds. However, bayberry is quite brittle. The addition of one part beeswax to two parts bayberry reduces the brittleness, increases the wax coverage on dipped candles, and sweetens the aroma. Because bayberry has a lower melting point than beeswax, use a wick one size smaller than you would for beeswax candles. (Too large a wick will cause dripping.) There is no need to add color or scent to bayberry candles — their earthy green color and newly mown-hay scent are part of the package!

BEESWAX

Beeswax is a secretion of honeybees. They use it to build the combs where they store their honey and incubate their larvae. When bees secrete wax, they shape it into the hexagonal shapes we associate with honeycombs. Amazingly, all bees, all over the world, have the ability to create hexagons with their wax — and each hexagon has angles within 3 to 4 degrees of each other! The layers of hexagons are offset from one another and result in the optimal use of space and engineered strength to allow 1 pound of hive wax to hold 22 pounds of honey. When beekeepers remove the honey for processing, they melt down the wax and sell it in blocks for cosmetics and candlemakers.

Beeswax has a wonderful sweet smell that varies depending on the type of plants and flowers on which the bees feed. Natural beeswax is golden yellow to brownish in color and contains bee and plant parts. It can be filtered to remove the impurities or bleached to a pure white, if desired. It is among the most desirable materials for candlemaking as it burns slowly with a beautiful golden glow and smells sweet. It can also be mixed with paraffin to create a more affordable but long-lasting candle.

CRACKING A SMILE

In days of old, beeswax was mixed with a lead compound and used as a base makeup on the faces of wealthy women to enhance their beauty. The women kept this white paste dry in the summer months by shielding the face from the sun with a fan. This way, the ladies could "save face." Of course, they were careful never to express mirth so they would not "crack a smile." And women who poked their noses into other people's business were told to "mind their own beeswax."

EARTH WAXES

Ozocerite, montan, and ceresines are waxes refined from coal, shale, and other fossilized earth fuels. They are used mostly as lubricants and polishes but are close to paraffin in chemical makeup.

PETROLEUM WAXES

Paraffins are the most commonly used waxes in candlemaking. They come in a variety of melting-point ranges. Paraffin is a by-product of the process of refining crude oil into motor oil. Crude oil is distilled into fractions, or cuts, in a pipe still. Crude oil is heated at the bottom of this tall pipe and separates according to temperature into heavy lubricating oil, light lubricating oil, fuel oil, and gasoline as it makes its way to hydrocarbon gas at the top. Waxes from light lubricating oils are chilled and sweated or distilled off, based on their melting points. These waxes are further refined through hydrogenation and end up with very specific properties.

Types: Generally, candlemaking paraffins are rated by melting point: low, medium, or high. Most candles require waxes with a melting point of 125° to 150°F. When you are purchasing wax from a craft store or from a candlemaking supplier, the wax will be labeled with its melting point and intended use. Most of the time, you will be adding stearic acid to the paraffin to increase its hardness and opacity.

Waxes are defined in the industry as fully refined (the kind you will be using for candlemaking), semi-refined (less expensive, less stable than fully refined), and scale waxes (darker in color and too soft to use for candles). The oil companies have divisions dedicated to different wax-refining methods for different industries. As candlemaking is alive and growing as a do-it-yourself craft, waxes are readily available at most craft stores, even in my small town.

If your candlemaking grows to the point where you need more than the 11-pound slabs generally sold in craft shops, the next size up is a 55-pound case. There are wax suppliers who will sell to the candle-maker wholesale with a minimum order of only 55 pounds, and once you go wholesale, new wax options become available to you. Much

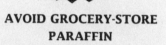

AVOID GROCERY-STORE PARAFFIN

Paraffin used for candles is not the same as what is sold in grocery stores as sealing wax for canning jars. This type of paraffin has a much lower melting point than candle wax and makes very soft, drippy candles. The only possible use for this wax in candlemaking could be in a container candle, but the wax would likely drown the wick by melting too fast.

information about wax, as about wick, is secret and proprietary, but as a wholesale customer, you can ask for a specifications sheet for any product, which will give you melting point and other information.

CUSTOM-BLENDED WAX

In response to the growing interest in candlemaking, many wax manufacturers have developed blended waxes, which are specifically formulated for making a certain type of candle. For example, taper-wax formulations already contain all of the ingredients needed to produce a durable, rigid candle with good adhesion between layers. And wax blends for molded candles can be formulated to pull away naturally from the walls of the mold, making it easier for you to remove it. Wax designed for container candles has low shrinkage, so it does not pull away from the walls of the container it is intended to fill. These specially formulated waxes have additives in them and should be used only for their intended purpose.

According to the folks who blend waxes, home candle manufacturers often make things harder for themselves by buying a custom blend and trying to change it into something it is not. Introducing other additives into custom-blended waxes may result in a very problematic wax. Before adding anything that changes the crystalline structure of a custom wax, try the wax as it is and determine whether it will work for you. It may be customized for a completely different use, and nothing you add will ever change that.

You should determine whether you're the kind of person who wants to buy a preformulated wax that you can melt and pour, or an adventurer who wants to make your own custom blends of waxes and additives by a process of experimentation, research, and development.

RECYCLED WAX

This is whatever you save in the way of candle butts, cheese coatings, sealing wax, chunks of stuff you chipped or melted out of the bottom of a votive cup, and candles you made that didn't quite work out. All of this can be reused to make new candles. Obviously, the weirder the mixture,

> "Instead of dirt and poison we have rather chosen
> to fill our hives with honey and wax; thus furnishing mankind with the two noblest of things, which are sweetness and light."
> —Jonathan Swift,
> The Battle of the Books

the less predictable the result, but if you're in the mood to experiment, this is the stuff to use. Even if you aren't saving strange waxes, please save all of your spills (have a putty knife nearby to scrape them up), mistakes, and leftover bits of colored wax that don't get used in a project. You can combine them, see what color they turn out, and darken or dilute the color to make what you like.

Recycle your candle butts into new candles.

SPERMACETI WAX

This is a waxy tissue found in the head cavities of sperm whales. The sperm whale *(Physeter catodon)* was originally named by whalers who thought that the fluid filling its head cavity was a reserve of semen. Although scientists are not certain, it is now believed that this white, waxy liquid acts as a lens to focus a whale's echolocation signals, which a whale uses for communication with other whales and for hunting prey.

Sperm whales can be up to 60 feet long, and their heads can be one-third that length to accommodate the spermaceti organ. The sperm whale was hunted extensively in the eighteenth and nineteenth centuries for its oil, its ambergris, and its spermaceti, which was made into long-burning, odorless candles. Spermaceti candles were highly prized because of the brightness of their light, their slightly sweet odor, and their long burning times. In fact, they were widely used to illuminate the lighthouses on the New England coast in the nineteenth century.

AMBERGRIS

In addition to producing spermaceti, the sperm whale is responsible for the substance known as ambergris. This fatty material is formed in the whale's intestinal tract. Fresh, it is black in color with an odor that's far from pleasant. When it's been dried by the sun, sea, and air, however, ambergris becomes a pleasantly fragrant yellow or gray mass that floats on water.

Ambergris is usually harvested in its dried form from the shores of China, Japan, Africa, the Americas, tropical islands, and the Bahamas. Some, however, still comes from dead or captured whales. It is commonly used as a fixative in perfume.

Spermaceti was the substance used in the candles that were employed to calibrate the Standard International Candle, a unit of light intensity that was used when incandescent lightbulbs came out in 1921. A Standard International Candle is the intensity of light emitted from a ⅙-pound spermaceti candle, burning at a rate of 120 grams per hour, duplicated in an incandescent lamp.

If spermaceti is available at all, it would be from specialty candle-making suppliers that import products from Europe.

GRANULATED WAX

Unlike wax sold in block form, granulated wax is processed into small beads. Paraffin, white beeswax, and many candle additives are sold in bead form and may be called granulated, beaded, prilled, or pastillated, depending on the size of the grains and the process used to create them. Historically, these beads have been used for the industrial manufacture of pressed candles (see page 12), but a more recent development in granulated wax is precoloring, a process that colors the beads thoroughly. This enables manufacturers to sell large quantities of colored wax beads to candle suppliers, who can repackage it into smaller (usually 1-pound) bags. It is sold under a variety of names, including granulated wax, magic wax crystals, and scented sand.

Since the granules are already dyed, they can be used to create layered candles in a process similar to sand art. These container candles require no melting of the wax material, so they are a good choice for candlemaking projects with children. Fragrance can be added to the wax beads; much like fragrance added to floral potpourri, it will adhere to the surface of each bead of wax. Simply place a rigid, tabbed wick into the container and distribute the beads of wax around the wick in any design you like. When you light the wick, it melts the granules to form a pool of wax.

TALLOW

There were three kinds of rendered animal fat used in candles before the nineteenth century — mutton fat from sheep, beef fat from cows, and pig fat. Of the three, mutton was considered the best and pig the worst. Mutton burned longer than the other two, tended not to smoke, and did not smell as bad. Pig, on the other hand, burned rapidly with a thick smoke and a foul smell.

VEGETABLE WAX

New "ecologically friendly" waxes are being introduced to augment the fossil (petroleum), animal (beeswax, tallow), and synthetic choices already available to candlemakers. While suppliers will not divulge their exact formulas, we do know that many of these products are soy based. As manufacturers hone their recipes, they are quickly creating a line of vegetable waxes with varied melting points that are designed for container, molded, and dipped candles.

You will have to rely on your wax supplier to get you started with the most appropriate wick for these new waxes. The softer, soy-based waxes are almost the consistency of soft soap or firm cream and, because of their all-natural ingredients, work as well in candles as they do in cosmetics. For candles requiring harder wax, there are also vegetable and paraffin blends, which offer the best that both plant and fossil fuels have to offer.

Candelilla and carnauba waxes are used primarily in wood and leather finishes. Candelilla is a reedlike plant covered by waxy scales native to northern Mexico and southern Texas. Carnauba is a fan-leaved palm native to Brazil. These waxes are brittle, are expensive, and have a high melting point, so they are used only in small quantities for candlemaking, in order to harden a softer wax (raise its melting point). Other vegetable waxes are also known but not commonly used in candlemaking.

If you're looking for all-vegetable waxes and/or stearic acid for kosher candles, be aware that these will not be commonly available from a craft store. Also be aware that unless the packaging clearly states that a wax or additive is all-vegetable, it probably isn't.

CANDLE GEL

Candle gel, trademarked by Penreco under the name Versagel C, is a late-20th-century candlemaking material that is a modern-day melding of the oil lamp and the candle; it isn't really a wax at all. The substance is composed of mineral oil and a patented polymer that gelatinizes the oil, turning it to a viscous, rubbery substance. The polymer allows the mineral oil to be solid at room temperature until the candle flame melts it into a combustible liquid.

Versagel C is available in three grades with three slightly different characteristics, so you will have to select one on the basis of your specific candlemaking plans. Versagel C LP is a low-polymer gel suitable for clear candles with low fragrance loads, typically 0 to 3 percent. Versagel C MP is a medium-polymer gel that can absorb medium to high fragrance loads of 3 to 5 percent, and Versagel C HP holds high fragrance loads and is dense enough to suspend pigments and decorative particles.

The advantages of candle gel include low shrinkage and good container adhesion, as well as the product's visual clarity and ability to hold up to 6 percent fragrance. The manufacturer claims that Versagel candles burn up to 5 times longer than comparably sized wax candles. Because it does not have a crystalline structure like regular wax, candle gel cannot stand on its own and must be used in a container.

Some people have concerns about the chemicals that may be emitted in the combustion of this product, but Penreco's tests indicate that the product has no adverse impact on indoor air quality, releasing hydrogen as it burns. It is important for you to run burn tests to find the proper wick size so that the candle creates a wax pool that is appropriate for its size and does not produce smoking and soot.

ADDITIVES

A number of substances can be added to wax when you want to achieve special effects in the appearance or characteristics of your candles. Additives work by modifying the crystalline structure of the candle wax, which may change the outward appearance of the candle as well as its melting point and burning properties. Similar additives are used in the cosmetics and food-service industries to produce specific qualities, be they visual or textural. In candlemaking, they are generally used at levels not exceeding 2 percent. Here are a few common ones.

STEARIC ACID

While not really an acid in the caustic sense we usually associate with acids, this candlemaking essential is an animal or vegetable fat refined to a flake or powder form. Its name comes from the Greek *stear,* meaning "solid fat, suet, or tallow."

CAUTION

Stearic acid is the most common candlemaking additive. It is almost always used with paraffin and rarely used with beeswax. It should never be used with rubber mold materials because it acts as a caustic. Nor should it be used with copper, because it acts as an oxidizer.

It is, in fact, a natural offshoot of the soapmaking craft. When fat is mixed with wood ashes (alkaline or lye), the chemical reaction produces soap and glycerin through the process of saponification. Mixing the soap with acid produces stearines. Chemical companies today still perform the same chemical reactions to produce soap, glycerin, and stearic acid from animal and vegetable fats.

Stearic acid causes two reactions when mixed with paraffin. It lowers its melting point and, when cooled, makes candles harder in order to prevent bending or slumping. The reaction between wax and stearic acid is remarkable because at critical percentages and temperatures, wax and stearic acid change their individual chemical structures to become one composition. Their combination creates a hard candle with an excellent, strong crystalline structure.

Stearic acid also makes otherwise translucent paraffin more opaque. Depending on what you're trying to do, you may want to reduce or eliminate the stearic acid from certain applications, such as overdipping a layer on top of flowers when you want the flowers to show through the translucence of the natural paraffin. Stearic acid is generally sold as Triple-Pressed Stearic Acid.

FISHER-TROPSCH (FT) WAX

This is a high-melt (215°F), synthetic paraffin wax made from coal gasification. You may find similar products marketed under names such as Translucent Crystals or Clear Sheen. These synthetic waxes promote a homogenous crystal structure in the wax, harden and raise the melting point of your candles, prevent surface mottling, and offer a translucent look to the wax without opacifying it as much as some of the other additives listed in this section. FT wax is often used to create candles with good glow through the wax. For example, this wax would be a good additive for a hurricane lamp, where you want the lamp to glow from within but be hard enough to not soften from the heat. Synthetic wax is also a good choice for pillar candles with surface decorations best illuminated from the inside.

VYBAR

Vybar, a polymerized olefin, is a popular candle additive that is often used to replace stearic acid. It improves the hardness of the candle without increasing brittleness (particularly important in taper candles) by promoting the growth of a smaller, more tightly woven network of crystals. This opacifies the wax to produce a consistent surface, eliminate bubbles, and increase the wax's ability to bind oil so that you can add more scent to your candle wax. One of its key benefits over many other additives is its relatively low melting point, which allows you to melt it along with the wax rather than melting it separately at a higher temperature and adding it to the melted wax later.

Vybar comes in two varieties: Vybar 103 (160°F-melting point) and Vybar 260 (130°F-melting point) and is sold in bead form. Select the Vybar product closest to the melting point of the wax you are using and start by using 1 percent by weight. According to Baker Petrolite, Vybar's manufacturer, adding 0.5 percent of Vybar makes it possible for wax to accept up to 5 percent fragrance. But don't overdo it; more than 2.5 percent is overkill and can cause smoking and other unforeseen problems.

POLYMERS

Polymers are synthetic additives that opacify the wax and enable you to achieve a nice, bright color without a mottled appearance. They have melting points above 200°F and, in general, must be melted separately from your wax, and then added and incorporated quickly, before they cool down. They are sold in block or bead form and are available in a variety of trade names, so you will have to rely on the supplier's description of their benefits to determine which one is right for you.

For instance, polyethylene polymer offers a higher degree of opacity than ethylene vinyl acetate co-polymer (AC-400), but AC-400 has a lower melting point, and you may find it easier to incorporate it into your wax. Again, it is best to begin by using 0.5 to 1 percent by weight and see what happens, because more is not necessarily better. Too much of a polymer can cause candles to smoke, may reduce burn diameter, or inhibit the wax from flowing through the wick.

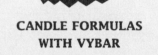

CANDLE FORMULAS WITH VYBAR

Note: If you are using Vybar or other additives to harden and opacify the paraffin, eliminate the stearic acid from these formulas.

WHITE PETROLATUM

This is the soft petroleum product we call Vaseline. It is the basic raw material used to make microcrystallines; in its soft, familiar form it may be used in container candles to reduce shrinkage, offer better adhesion to the glass walls of the container, and increase oil retention of fragrances without allowing them to bleed out. White petrolatum is also used in sculptable waxes to keep them soft.

MICROCRYSTALLINES

These are refined from de-oiled petrolatum and are engineered by the manufacturer to offer many different benefits to the candlemaker, including better layer adhesion between dips and increased tackiness for wax-to-wax adhesion of modeling wax. There are two basic kinds of microcrystalline waxes used by the candlemaker: the soft, pliable kind, which is used to increase the elasticity of wax, and the hard, brittle type, which increases the durability of candles. The soft microcrystallines make wax tacky and malleable for sculpting and carving. The hard microcrystallines tend to make candles more forgiving and resilient, with less cracking and chipping. Generally, they are used in higher percentages than the synthetic additives, usually 5 to 15 percent.

Your candle supplier may offer only one or two microcrystallines, but in reality there are at least 50 types of microcrystallines on the market. They are all very similar but have slightly different effects on wax. You will have to rely on the supplier's description of the product's benefits to determine which one is right for you.

When you peruse a candle supplier's list of additives, most of them will be listed with a trade name and a description of the impact they will have on your candle wax. It may be difficult for you to ascertain whether you are buying synthetic wax, polymer, or microcrystalline, and it probably doesn't matter. The bottom line is this: If you are making a particular kind of candle without additives and running into a problem that might be eliminated by using them, give them a try, making sure to follow the manufacturer's directions for recommended percentages and melting temperature. Always start with a small amount and increase the quantity as needed.

However, it is important to remember that anything you add may introduce as many quirks as it eliminates. This is where the kitchen chemistry of candlemaking comes in. Be prepared to make a series of candles using your chosen wick, color, and scent but each with a different percentage of the additive. Then do side-by-side comparisons of color, surface texture, aromatic qualities, and burn characteristics. This may seem like a lot of work, and it is. But if you plan to sell your candles, you will want to achieve consistent, reproducible results. It's worth taking the time to do your research and development up front.

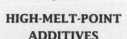

HIGH-MELT-POINT ADDITIVES

When you are using additives with high melting points (over 180°F), you may find it helpful to melt the additive separately before adding it to your candle wax. The additive's high melting point can make it difficult to completely incorporate it into a large quantity of lower-melt-point wax.

High-melt-point additives will incorporate more easily into your large batch of candle wax if they are first blended with a small quantity of candle wax when you melt it. To do this, mix an equal quantity of your candle wax with the additive and melt this mixture separately from your larger candlemaking batch. Crank up the temperature on the additive mixture to fully melt it. When it is melted, add it to your larger batch of candle wax; the two mixtures should blend nicely.

ADDITIVES

Additive	Melting Point	Recommended Percentage	Common Trade Names and/or Manufacturer
FT Wax	215°F	0–2%	Translucent Crystals, Clear Sheen
Vybar 103	160°F	0–2%	Baker Petrolite
Vybar 260	130°F	0–2%	Baker Petrolite
Polyethylene	185–260°F	0–2	Opaque Crystals, Clear Crystals
Ethylene Vinyl Acetate Co-Polymer	198°F	0–2%	AC-400, Elvax
White Petrolatum	130–175°F	2–40%	Vaseline, Penreco, Witco
Micro-crystallines (soft)	50–180°F	2–30%	Cut and Curl, Tacky Micro, Victory, Multiwax
Micro-crystallines (hard)	165–200°F	2–15%	Be Square

DO YOU REALLY NEED AN ADDITIVE?

Don't assume that additives are the answer to all of your candlemaking problems. Most problems can be solved by finding the right wax for the type of candle you are making, selecting the right wick for the type of wax you have chosen, and controlling the temperature of the wax as you make your candles. The vast majority of home candlemakers get by with wax, wick, and possibly one additive, such as stearic acid or Vybar.

Don't misunderstand me — additives play an important role in the candlemaking industry, enabling waxes to be modified visually and texturally for different purposes. But the purist in me urges you to try making candles without a lot of unnecessary additives. In the long run, the fewer unknowns you introduce into your recipe, the cleaner burning your candle will be.

Opt to use additives only after you have exhausted the variables of wax, wick, and environmental conditions that are the most likely causes of your troubles. The exercise of developing a tried and true candle formulation will be well worth it, since you'll learn about the nuances of working with wax and, ultimately, you'll make the best candle with the fewest ingredients.

WAX FORMULAS

The wax and wick specified in this book's recipes are guidelines to get you started. For successful candles, you must remember that the relationship among a wax's melting point, the selected wick type and size, and a finished candle's diameter is critical in determining the burning characteristics of a finished product. Remember to take notes so that you can repeat your successes or make adjustments for your next batch of candles.

While many recipes offer formulas in teaspoons and tablespoons, I find this difficult to work with. For example, stearic acid comes in powder and flake forms, and a teaspoon of flake weighs a lot less than a teaspoon of powder because of the difference in density. For more accuracy, I offer formulas by weight or by ratio.

SHEET WAX

One pound of wax will make approximately four sheets of wax, enough for four 10- by 1-inch candles.

Formula A
1 pound (454 g) of beeswax

Formula B
½ pound (227 g) of beeswax
½ pound (227 g) of paraffin with a 130–150°F melting point

Formula C (if you're not using beeswax)
9 parts paraffin
1 part stearic acid, optional

ADDING BEESWAX

The addition of beeswax to candle formulas increases a candle's burn time and the pliability of the wax. It also increases the possibility of wax sticking to a mold, so be sure to use mold release!

POURED AND DIPPED CANDLES

There is a wide variety of formulas that can be used to make poured or dipped candles.

Formula A
Paraffin with 5 to 30 percent stearic acid (I like 10 to 15 percent)

Formula B
6 parts paraffin
3 parts stearic acid
1 part beeswax

Formula C
85 percent paraffin
10 percent stearic acid
5 percent candelilla wax or 3 percent carnauba wax for strength

Formula D
Paraffin and beeswax mixed in any proportion

Church candles are made with the above formula using a greater proportion of beeswax to paraffin. While the proportion of beeswax used to be higher, 52 percent beeswax with 48 percent paraffin is the current mix for church candles.

Formula E
60 percent paraffin
35 percent stearic acid
5 percent beeswax

This is a recipe from an old book for making "Standard Commercial Candles."

MODELING WAX

This wax is used for sculpting and rolling candles.

1 part paraffin		3 parts paraffin		2 parts beeswax
1 part beeswax	OR	1 part microcrystalline	OR	1 part paraffin
		(for pliability)		

SCULPTING/PASTE WAX

This wax can be used to make shapes to decorate candles.

2 pounds (908 g) of beeswax
3 ounces (85 g) of white petrolatum

PAINTING WAX

This wax can be applied with a brush.

4 parts beeswax
1 part turpentine

TALLOW CANDLES

Most candlemakers never try their hand at this traditional candlemaking wax. But if you do, here's a recipe to get you started.

2 pounds (908 g) of tallow
1 pound (454 g) of beeswax
6 ounces (170 g) of stearic acid
2 tablespoons (30 ml) of scent

How Much Wax Will You Need?

Dipping: You will need at least 6 pounds (2.7 kg) of wax to dip three pairs of 10- by ⅞-inch tapers, more if your dipping can is very wide-mouthed. Only about half this wax will become candle — the rest is only there to give you the depth you need to completely submerge the wicks.

Container or Molded Candles: There are two ways to determine the amount of wax needed for container or molded candles. First, pour water into your mold or container, or into a plastic bag inserted into your mold if you want to keep the mold dry right before pouring wax into it. Measure that amount of water in a measuring cup, determining its volume, then convert this volume to pounds by using the conversion chart at right. For example, if your container holds 4 cups of water, you will need approximately 2 pounds of wax. (Remember, extra wax is never wasted. It can be cooled and stored for your next candlemaking adventure.)

Or, if you are using the double-boiler method to melt your wax and have scored the inside of your melting pot to mark the incremental depths of different weights of wax (see page 58), simply pour the water from your mold into your melting pot to see which line it reaches. This will quickly tell you how many pounds of wax you need.

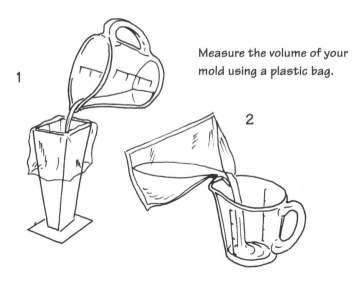

1

2

Measure the volume of your mold using a plastic bag.

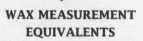

WAX MEASUREMENT EQUIVALENTS

Once you know approximately how much wax you need to fill a mold or to dip some candles, you will need to convert your wax formula to the units of measurements most convenient for the container or method you are using. Following are some of the more common equivalency measurements.

◆ 1½ cups (355 ml) of melted wax = approximately 1 pound (454 g) of solid wax

◆ 12 fluid ounces (355 ml) of melted wax = approximately 1 pound (454 g) of solid wax

◆ 1 gallon (3.76 ml) = 4 quarts = 8 pints = 16 cups

◆ 1 cup (237 ml) = 8 fluid ounces

◆ 1 pint (473 ml) = 16 fluid ounces

◆ 1 pound = 16 ounces = 454 grams (pounds x 16 = ounces; pounds x 454 = grams)

◆ 1 ounce = 28.35 grams (ounces x 28.35 = grams)

The Basic Math of Wax

When making candles, the weight of the wax and additives is important for the recipe but the volume is important for figuring the space the wax will fill, or the depth to which a can will allow a candle to be dipped. Each wax is slightly different in its proportion of weight to volume, but here are some guidelines:

An Example

Sample conversion. Let's assume you're going to make a molded candle that requires 6 pounds (2.7 kg) from the following 10-pound (4.5 kg) formula:

> 6 parts paraffin
> 3 parts stearic acid
> 1 part beeswax

1. There are 10 parts called for in this formula: 6 (paraffin) + 3 (stearic acid) + 1 (beeswax) = 10. Since you need only 6 pounds (2.7 kg) or $^6/_{10}$ of the total formula, begin by figuring: 6 ÷ 10 = .6

2. Now multiply each part of the formula by .6.

> 6 parts paraffin x .6 = 3.6 pounds (1.6 kg) of paraffin
> 3 parts stearic acid x .6 = 1.8 pounds (817 g) of stearic acid
> 1 part beeswax x .6 = .6 pounds (272 g) of beeswax

Therefore, to make 6 pounds of candles, you need 3.6 pounds (1.64 kg) of paraffin, 1.8 pounds (817 g) of stearic acid, and .6 pounds (272 g) of beeswax.

Another example. Let's say you need a total of 6 pounds of wax and your formula calls for 85 percent paraffin and 15 percent stearic acid.

You can figure out the amount of wax and additives by multiplying the total quantity of material needed by the percentage called for in the recipe.

To find the 85 percent paraffin you need for a total of 6 pounds (2.7 kg) of material, figure: .85 x 6 = 5.1 pounds (2.3 kg).

To find the 15 percent stearic acid you need for a total of 6 pounds of material, figure: .15 x 6 = .9 pounds (408 g).

Converting Teaspoons and Tablespoons

If you start with a recipe that calls for teaspoons or tablespoons, you can convert this from volume to weight by weighing the number of spoonfuls called for in the recipe and multiplying or dividing this weight by the same factor by which you multiply or divide your wax to reach your desired total. This is especially useful if you are making a larger quantity of candles and don't want to count out the total amount of stearic acid one tablespoon at a time.

A common candlemaking recipe calls for 3 tablespoons (44 ml) of stearic acid to a pound (454 g) of paraffin. You can weigh 3 tablespoons of stearic acid and, using simple math conversions, figure out how many grams or ounces you need per pound of paraffin. Since stearic acid comes in flake and powder forms, this weight will be different for each. If you prefer, you can measure 3 tablespoons for each pound of paraffin you use.

ADDITIVE GUIDELINES

The Oran Wax Company suggests that when you add any other substances to wax, always start with the smallest amount and work your way up. Keep in mind that the two most important factors for success in using additives are: (1) the precise measurement of the additive, and (2) the correct mixing and blending of the additive with wax. Add the **precise amount** of additive to clear melted wax and stir until all of the individual pieces have completely melted, **then stir for an additional 3 minutes.** Or, melt the correct amount of additive with a small amount of wax in a separate container. When this is completely melted, slowly add it to your molten wax, **stirring constantly for at least 3 minutes!**

In case you are feeling overwhelmed at this point, let me add that for making most candles, you will need only wick, wax, stearic acid, color and scent if you choose, and the equipment outlined in chapter 5.

ORAN WAX COMPANY ADDITIVE PERCENTAGE CHART

The Oran Wax Company offers the following chart to aid the candlemaker in figuring out small percentages, ⅛ percent to 5 percent, for various quantities of wax. You may find it useful for figuring additives, scents, and colorants, too.

Pounds of wax	⅛%	¼%	½%	1%	2%	5%
1	.02	.04	.08	.16	.32	.80
2	.04	.08	.16	.32	.64	1.60
3	.06	.12	.24	.48	.96	2.40
4	.08	.16	.32	.64	1.28	3.20
5	.10	.20	.40	.80	1.60	4.00
6	.12	.24	.48	.96	1.92	4.80
7	.14	.28	.56	1.12	2.24	5.60
8	.16	.32	.64	1.28	2.56	6.40
9	.18	.36	.72	1.44	2.88	7.20
10	.20	.40	.80	1.60	3.20	8.00
11	.22	.44	.88	1.76	3.52	8.80
22	.44	.88	1.76	3.52	7.04	17.60
44	.88	1.76	3.52	7.04	14.08	35.20
50	1.00	2.00	4.00	8.00	16.00	40.00
55	1.10	2.20	4.40	8.80	17.60	44.00
60	1.20	2.40	4.80	9.60	19.20	48.00
100	2.00	4.00	8.00	16.00	32.00	80.00

CHAPTER 4
Color and Scent

Two of the attributes that we most commonly associate with candles are rich colors and pleasing scents. This is an area of candlemaking where you can have great fun experimenting with the endless possibilities.

ADDING COLOR

In large-scale candlemaking operations, coloring is done with powdered dyes or dyes dissolved in xylene solvent. These colorants are so concentrated that in many cases, less than 1 gram will color 10 pounds of wax. The dye powders are so finely ground that users must wear a dust mask or respirator to prevent inhalation. For this reason, I wouldn't recommend them to the home candlemaker even if they were commonly available.

Many professional candlemakers use aniline dyes, which are soluble in waxes and oils, to color their wax. For the home candle crafter, these are the best color option available. They are conveniently sold as color blocks, disks, or chips.

Candle colors will fade over time, particularly pinks and purples. There are ultraviolet inhibitors available in the industry to prevent this, and they may be purchased in small quantity through a candle-craft supplier. However, the best ways to prevent fading are to store candles out of direct light and to burn them before they get old and faded! Candles aren't for saving, they're for using. The same advice applies to scented candles.

I encourage those of you who enjoy natural dyeing to experiment with materials such as herb leaves, beets, onion skins, coffee grounds, and curry powders to color candles. Bear in mind that candle color must be oil soluble, so you

Natural materials can be used to color wax and can then be removed.

47

won't be able to use water or alcohol to extract the color from the plant material. Steep the vegetable matter in oil or melted wax and expect relatively pastel colors.

Colors without Limits

Don't feel limited by the color disks available at your supplier. These are just a start. Wax colors can be blended together to achieve any hue you desire. The basic color wheel can help you get started. Primary colors (red, yellow, and blue) can be blended to make the secondary colors (orange, green, and purple).

COLOR BLENDING GUIDE		
Primary Colors		**Secondary Color**
red + yellow	=	orange
yellow + blue	=	green
blue + red	=	purple

The addition of a color's complement, its opposite on the color wheel, tends to gray or mute the primary color. The addition of a small amount of black creates a darker shade of the starting color.

A whitener is sold for opaque pastels that acts to whiten the dyes so you can achieve opacity of color and still use a minute quantity of dye. For very light, subtle colors, you can use just a small amount of dye, without whitener, and the candle will be pastel and translucent.

Mixing more than two colors together will often result in interesting red-browns. Since red seems to be the most powerful wax color, most recycled blends of wax turn out reddish brown.

Conserving Dye

If you know that you're going to decorate, use little or no dye in the candle to be decorated (also called a core candle) and make intensely colored wax paints or sheets or overdips for the surface.

Since you will always have wax left over from making candles, making colors you can reuse is a good idea. It's almost impossible to melt just the right amount, and for dipped candles you'll have to melt more than you need just to fill the dipping pot. Five pounds of leftover bright orange wax isn't nearly as versatile as 5 pounds of white.

BALANCE THE RECIPE!

You may be tempted to use additives to intensify the color or scent of your candles. There's nothing wrong with that, but you have to go into it with your eyes open. Additives change the structure of the wax, allowing it to reflect light differently (changing the color intensity), bind an increased amount of oil (making a stronger scent), or increase the melting point (becoming more durable). At the same time, the change in wax structure may have an impact on the candle's burning properties.

The art of candlemaking, enhanced and complicated by wax technology, synthetic additives, wick options, and scent and color choices, is like cooking — each ingredient changes the overall product, and adding anything new may necessitate modifications to the whole recipe. Instead of taste testing, we candlemakers burn test to check the flame's size and consistency, the emission of smoke, the size of the wax pool, whether the candle drips, and whether the wick is able to combust all of the wax.

As you can see, there is much more to candlemaking than simply how the candle looks!

ULTRAVIOLET INHIBITOR

This additive helps reduce color fading of candle dyes, which occurs naturally as candles are exposed to light. In general, candles should be stored in the dark. Obviously, this is not possible when you are displaying them, but candles should never be exhibited in bright, direct sunlight, which exposes them to ultraviolet rays and heat, which can distort them.

Over time, you will be able to determine whether the dyes you have chosen have a tendency to fade; some colors fade more quickly than others. UV Inhibitor helps preserve candle color under normal conditions and is used in small quantities (1 teaspoon per pound of wax). For candles that are colored through and through, UV Inhibitor can be added to the entire batch of candle wax.

For white candles with a colored overdip, UV Inhibitor can be added to the colored overdip wax. In my experience, the thinner the coating of colored wax, the more severe the change in color. Under these conditions, UV inhibitor can help retard the natural fading of candle dyes.

SCENTING CANDLES

Historically, the use of scent in candles began with beeswax and bayberry, which are naturally scented. Nowadays, there are many options available for scenting your living space, ranging from wholly natural herb potpourris to completely synthetic air fresheners.

There are many scent options in the candle business as well. You can purchase candle fragrance oils through a craft store. These are generally synthetic concentrates known in the trade as industrial odorants. You can also explore the essential oil market, which has become more popular since the onset of aromatherapy. The perfume industry also offers concentrates of various base scents as well as licensed mixtures. Be sure you use scents that are oil-based, not alcohol-based, since alcohol will evaporate quickly in hot wax.

One of the most common complaints among candlemakers is that it is difficult to scent a candle so that the aroma lasts. Many non-candle scent formulations volatilize (dissipate into the air), either as soon as the scent is put into the hot wax or over time at room temperature, before the candle is lit. If the scent's chemical makeup causes it to dissipate at a temperature lower than the melting point of the wax, chances are that you will have unscented wax by the time it cools (though it will smell great while you're making the candles). I encourage you to experiment, but go into it with your eyes open; if the scent evaporates upon contact with hot wax, it will not produce a scented candle.

Scents that have been specifically formulated for candlemaking are designed to withstand the high temperatures necessary to melt the wax. The challenge for candlemakers is to find aromas that smell natural despite the fact that they are synthetic, and to create a balanced recipe in which the amount of scent does not cause the candle to smoke.

In general, candle wax cannot hold more than 2 to 3 percent scent. More than that amount will cause the scented oil to ooze out through the candle's surface, because it has not really joined in a chemical bond with the wax. In fact, using the wrong scent or too much scent can result in smoke emissions and the production of soot, an indoor air problem (see Indoor Air Quality, page 133).

For most scents, however, 2 to 3 percent is plenty. But some scents are weaker than others are, and you may want to increase the percentage of scent to create a more aromatic candle. To allow you this option, there are candle additives designed to increase your wax's ability to bind oils, which enables you to increase the percentage of scent you can use per pound of wax. You'll have to decide whether to find a stronger scent or use additives to allow you to add a higher percentage of a scent you know to be weak.

Your candle supplier's catalog will recommend percentages for their scents and will list the benefits of each additive so that you can determine which ones may increase your wax's ability to bind scent. But remember — additives change the crystalline structure of the wax, and while you may find one that allows you to add more scent, it may also change the melting point of your wax, which may, in turn, force you to use a different wick! Each ingredient in your candle recipe must be chosen not only for its individual benefits but also for its interaction with the other ingredients.

Essential Oils

Because of the temperature of a candle's flame and the volatility of essential oils, you may find that adding essential oils to candle wax does not guarantee you will smell them when the candle burns. To overcome this problem, commercially made candle scents contain fixatives and stabilizers, which cause the odor to remain longer and to become activated with the heat of a flame. Many of these products are synthetics, however, leaving some to seek a natural alternative.

To produce more fragrance when a candle burns, some people soak their wicks in essential oils. You can also add a drop or two of scent to a burning candle's molten wax pool. Depending on the chemical composition of the scent, the flame may or may not pick up the fragrance.

Be aware that essential oils are fuel for a candle's flame and will dissipate quickly. If you put drops of oil on a cold candle and then light it, the oil will be burned before the wax and may make your candle smoke.

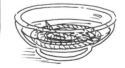

Candles can be scented by soaking the wick in essential oil or adding a drop or two of oil to the wax pad.

In addition to trying essential oils, experiment with these readily available products: vanilla beans, the oil of cloves sold at many pharmacies, scented bath oils, solid-stick colognes, and any other oil-based, scented product. Some scents tend to evaporate as the candle sits out in the air, while others are activated by the heat of the flame, but you won't know what will work until you try.

Even if a candle's flame doesn't pick up the scent of an essential oil as it burns, the scented wax of a cold candle will disperse in a room. And when a friend opens your Christmas gift of cinnamon-scented candles, it makes the treat just that much nicer.

Adding Essential Oil to Wax

A general starting-point formula for scent is ½ teaspoon of essential oil per pound of wax. Because the addition of oils will change the chemical makeup of wax, you should not use more than 3 percent oil by weight. If you do, the surface of your candle may be mottled, or worse, the oil might ooze out of the candle.

If you need to use more than 3 percent in order to make a candle fragrant, the oil you are using is not concentrated enough to be used for candles.

How Essential Oils Are Obtained

While fixed oils, such as butter and tallow, do not evaporate, essential oils are volatile oils that do evaporate, particularly when exposed to heat. Used for their flavor and odor, volatile oils are extracted from an aromatic plant — from the flowers, bark, buds, seeds, leaves, rinds, roots, and/or wood, or, in some cases, the whole plant. In commercial production, there are three methods of extracting these volatile oils.

Steam distillation. The oils are extracted by using steam to volatilize them into a gas, which is then condensed to a liquid by cooling. This is

POTPOURRI CANDLES

One candlemaker recommends rolling a warm pillar or sphere candle in potpourri and then overdipping it so that it has a layer of actual flower petals and leaves just under its surface. As with all other aspects of candlemaking, creativity and a willingness to exercise trial and error are important.

ADDING HERBAL SCENTS

Powdered or dried herbs can be used to scent wax. These can be strained out by filtering the hot wax through interfacing or left in to create an interesting color and texture in the wax. If you decide to leave the herbs in the wax, be aware that a burning candle may create the smell of burning herbs, not herbal fragrance, as the wax melts.

Filter any solids out of wax by using interfacing fabrics.

a highly industrialized method requiring many, many pounds of plant material to yield results. For example, it takes 12,000 pounds of jasmine flowers to make 2 pounds of oil this way.

Enfleurage. In the enfleurage method, flower petals are placed on a glass and covered with fat. The fat absorbs the fragrant oils of the petals. This is called a pomade, which is used to make creams and salves. Pomades can also be treated with alcohol to dissolve the fat and leave the essential oil behind.

Solvent extraction. Plant material is placed in ethyl alcohol, and the essential oil rises to the top. The solution is then chilled and the oils are removed from the surface, like fat from soup stock.

COMMON SCENTS FOR YOUR CANDLES

Essential oils, whether made from plants in your garden or purchased commercially, offer a wide variety of fragrance choices for candles. Here is a list of scents based on one developed by Susan Miller Cavitch for *The Natural Soap Book* (Storey Communications, Inc.). It's divided by scent families to get you started thinking about making fragrant candles. Keep in mind that an overpowering aroma can be very irritating, no matter how much you like the scent in moderation. Aim for subtle, suggestive scents that whisper rather than shout.

Floral

Carnation
Gardenia
Honeysuckle
Lavender
Mimosa
Ylang-ylang
Hyacinth
Chamomile
Lilac
Jasmine
Rose
Geranium
Apple blossom
Lily
Iris
Jonquil

Citrus

Bee balm
Lemon balm
Lemon
Orange
Lime
Verbena

Woody

Bayberry
Sandalwood
Cedar
Patchouli
Rosewood
Juniper berry
Pine
Thyme

Spicy

Cinnamon
Cloves
Ginger
Mint
Nutmeg
Basil
Vanilla

Herbal

Rosemary
Marjoram
Dill
Tarragon
Coriander
Fennel
Caraway seed
Clary sage

MAKING YOUR OWN SCENTS

You can also extract your own scents from fresh herbs. Harvest them in the early morning, just after the dew has evaporated. Flowers should be picked just as they are beginning to bloom. To use citrus peels, scrape off and discard the white inner pulp. Steam distillation is not an option for home extraction of essential oils. I recommend the following versions of the enfleurage and solvent extraction methods.

Wax Infusion Method

Since paraffin is a form of oil, it can be used to extract essential oils, as follows.

1. Immerse flowers, leaves, roots, and/or branches in hot wax by hanging them in the wax in a muslin bag, or put them directly into the wax. Keep the wax temperature at 20 degrees above its melting point for at least 45 minutes.

2. If you have put the herbs directly in the wax, filter the mixture through medium-weight interfacing (used in sewing and available in fabric and craft shops). This works well if the herb particles are tiny because it will filter out small impurities. Or, if the particles are large, filter with a piece of muslin.

In addition to adding fragrance to your wax (and kitchen), the infusion will also dye the wax slightly, usually to a beautiful pastel sage green if you are using leaves. The scent will be very subtle and may not be present when you burn the candle.

3. You can repeat the infusion process over and over using the same wax with a new bundle of herbs each time, or, as recommended in many candlemaking books, augment the scent with a commercially produced fragrance.

MY ROSEMARY STORY

Like many other people, I love the scent of fresh rosemary and decided to try my hand at adding this delightful fragrance to a batch of candles. Once my wax was melted and 20°F above its melting point, I added fresh sprigs from my garden and let the mixture steep for hours.

My house was filled with the smell of the herb, and I eagerly anticipated burning the tapers I made with the wax. Imagine my disappointment when I lit my first rosemary candle and discovered all its scent had dissipated in the infusion. However, the wax was a beautiful shade of sage green.

Ah well, you just never know until you try.

Oil Infusion Method

Scent can also be extracted with oil. You can use olive or safflower oil for this process, but professionals recommend jojoba or turkey red oil, available through herb and perfume suppliers, because they are less likely to discolor or go rancid. If you are making a small quantity that you plan to use within a year, rancidity is probably not an issue as long as you store the oil in a cool place. Perform the following steps:

1. Bruise the herbs by mashing them with a spoon. Using a nonmetallic container, cover the herbs with oil for at least 24 hours.
2. Strain the oil, pressing it through the leaves so they will release any leftover oil.
3. Repeat this process with the same oil at least six times, to achieve a higher concentration. You can then use the oil to scent candles or in potpourri, as a room scent, or for body perfume.

Solvent Extraction Method

Remember, alcohol will evaporate in hot wax, so your solvent extraction will need to be chilled and the oil skimmed from its surface.

1. Cover the herbs with ethyl (not rubbing) alcohol, vodka, or a tasteless, high-proof alcohol called Everclear.
2. Repeat the process described for the oil infusion method above at least six times.
3. You can use this extraction as is for making perfume or toilet water, but for candlemaking you'll have to remove the oil from the alcohol by placing the mixture in the freezer. The oil will solidify on top of the alcohol and can be skimmed off.

CHAPTER 5
Equipment

The equipment you use for candlemaking should be dedicated to wax work only. Once these implements are used for candlemaking, they will be craft tools forever, never again to be used in cooking. Even the large pot you use to boil water will probably get wax in it, and although you could remove the wax with great diligence, you probably won't want to bother.

The equipment lists in this chapter cover everything you need to make sheet, poured, and dipped candles, but not every item is necessary to make candles. Before you begin to collect or buy equipment for candlemaking, please read this chapter thoroughly so you'll know just what you need to make the kinds of candles you want. The materials and equipment necessary for each type of candle are listed at the beginning of each set of candlemaking instructions.

CAUTION

Whenever you heat wax to its melting point, be sure not to heat it beyond its burning point. When speaking of wax, burning point means the temperature at which the properties of that particular wax have been stretched. Most paraffin waxes should not get hotter than 200°F.

Also be aware that most waxes, including beeswax, have a flashpoint, the temperature at which they will combust. The flashpoint of most waxes is 440°F. Never leave wax unattended when you're heating it, and be sure to have an accurate thermometer to monitor its temperature.

WAX-MELTING SYSTEMS

There are two types of wax-melting systems: a double boiler or a concealed element heater. They are equally effective and the choice is up to you.

Double-Boiler System

The double-boiler arrangement includes three components: a large outer pot to boil water; a smaller, inner pot in which to melt wax; and a trivet, or three-point stand, for the smaller pot to sit on. For the outer pot, choose a heavy-duty vessel large enough to contain an amount of water to reach at least two-thirds of the way up the sides of your melting pot. The water pot must have a trivet, or a three-point stand, for the melting pot to sit on. In place of a trivet, you can use three shallow tin cans filled with water so they don't float, or bend wire mesh into a raised trivet

MARKING THE MELTING POT

Put a pound of wax into your melting pot. After it melts, make a permanent mark inside the can at the level of the wax by scoring it with an awl or other pointed instrument. This is the 1-pound mark. Repeat this melting and marking process with 2, 3, 4, and 5 pounds of wax. Every time you use your melting pot, you will know approximately how much melted wax is in it by looking at your marks.

shape. The wax-melting pot should be metal and shaped so that you can pour from it. A metal pitcher with a handle is ideal, or you can use a large can such as an olive oil can and ladle out the wax instead of pouring it. When you use the double-boiler method to melt wax, you must replenish the water as it boils down in order to maintain a level as high up the sides of the wax pot as possible.

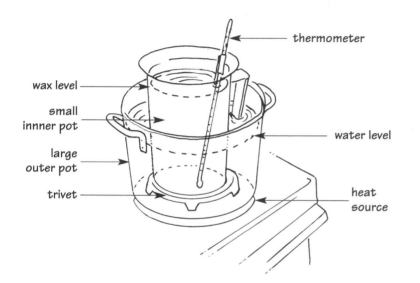

thermometer

wax level

small innner pot

large outer pot

trivet

water level

heat source

Double-boiler wax-melting setup

Concealed-Element Heater

A deep-fat fryer, slow-cooker, or other concealed-element heater allows you to heat wax directly in the pot since it will not come into contact with the heat source. The drawback to this method is that you cannot pour wax directly from a concealed-element heater. Instead, you'll have to ladle out hot wax into a pouring device.

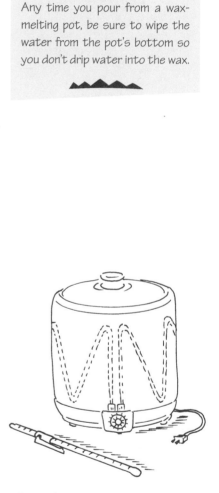

Concealed-element heater for melting wax, and a thermometer

Your heater must have an accurate, numbered (not low-medium-high) temperature control that can be set as low as 150°F. You can also use this heater to heat water, and set into the water a wax-melting pot exactly like the one outlined in the double boiler method. As with the double-boiler method, you must remember to replenish the water frequently.

Other Essential Equipment

In addition to a wax-melting system, you will need the following basic pieces of equipment.

◆ **Thermometer.** Your thermometer should be able to measure 0–300°F and clip to the inside of your wax pot so that enough of it is submerged in the wax to give you an accurate reading.

   The instructions in this book are given in degrees Fahrenheit. If your thermometer is in centigrade, use the chart below to convert this information.

◆ **Ladle.** Select one that gives you a comfortable angle when you transfer hot melted wax from one place to another.

◆ **Metal dipping can.** At least 12 inches deep for dipping tapers. If the wax-melting pot you are using for the double-boiler melting method is deep enough, you can use it as a dipping can. You can also use a large, rectangular olive oil can.

◆ **Kraft paper, foil, or waxed paper.** Be sure to have plenty on hand to cover and protect work surfaces.

ESSENTIALS FOR YOUR WORK AREA

◆ A level work surface
◆ Access to water
◆ A heat source (preferably not an open flame)

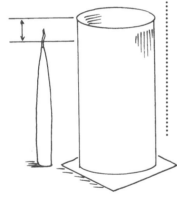

Use a dipping can 2 inches deeper than your longest candle.

A HANDY TEMPERATURE CONVERSION CHART

°C = (5⁄9 × °F) - 32
°F = (9⁄5 × °C) + 32
1 degree centigrade = 1.8 degrees Fahrenheit
1 degree Fahrenheit = .56 degrees centigrade

- **Spouted metal pitcher.** This is ideal to pour wax from and keep wax hot in. A pitcher may be your wax-melting pot or it may be the vessel into which you ladle melted wax.
- **Scissors.** For cutting wick.
- **Razor blades or sharp knife.** Used to cut wax sheets for rolled candles and to trim seam lines from molded candles.
- **Metal straightedge.** Used in cutting wax sheets for rolled candles. If you can find a straightedge longer than 1 foot, this will be a great help when cutting diagonal lines across sheet wax, as this measurement is greater than 12 inches.
- **Suitable cutting surface.** A heavy board or a mat that will withstand pressure from a sharp knife or razor blade.
- **Bucket.** Choose one large enough to hold the water necessary to cool your molds.
- **Pot holders.** Be sure to keep pot holders or heat mitts nearby to protect your hands.
- **Scale.** Your scale should have a range of zero to at least 10 pounds. It's handy, but not necessary, if your scale has a knob that will recalibrate its weight back to zero after you place your measuring container on it. This way, you won't have to subtract the weight of the container from the total of the ingredients being measured.

  The scale will be used to weigh wax, stearic acid, and other additives. For more precise measurement for materials such as color and scent, you might want a scale that is accurate to 1 gram.
- **Weights, both large and small.** An old barbell, a brick, or a piece of heavy scrap metal are used to keep a wax-filled mold submerged in water. Smaller weights, such as washers, nuts, and curtain weights, are needed to dangle from the end of a wick when making dipped candles.
- **Dowel, chopstick, or skewer.** These are useful for puncturing or piercing the surface of molded candles before you repour.
- **Masking tape or mold sealer.** Used to hold the wick in place.

A spouted metal pitcher is an essential tool.

Weighing your ingredients makes candlemaking more successful.

CAUTION

Do not use newspaper to cover your work surface. Wax and heat will cause the print to transfer to your countertops!

- **Hammer.** For breaking the wax blocks into smaller pieces.
- **Oil or mold-release spray.** Vegetable oil or commercially available mold-release spray will keep wax from sticking to your store-bought or handmade molds. You can safely use vegetable oil on any kind of mold, by either wiping some on with a paper towel or using the spray-on type. Do not overdo this! Too much oil will result in a mottled surface effect on your candle.

  Many moldmakers recommend silicone spray mold release, available where you buy the mold. It is quite effective. Many of the silicone rubber and RTV (room temperature vulcanizing) molds have a natural tendency to release from wax — they always have an oily feel to them and need little or no additional mold release. If you are using a disposable mold, you can choose not to use mold release, since you can cut and peel the mold off the candle rather than having to release the candle from the mold.
- **Paint scraper or putty knife.** Useful for cleaning up spilled wax.
- **Paper towels.** For spreading oil, mopping up water, and lots of other chores.
- **Nylon panty hose.** Perfect for polishing new candles or reviving old ones. Once I get a run in my panty hose, I cut them into rag-sized lengths and save them for candle polishing.

Not-So-Essential but Handy-to-Have Equipment

- **Blow-dryer or heating pad.** Useful for heating containers or molds and to keep wax sheets pliable.
- **Cake pans or cookie sheets.** Great to set containers of melted wax on.
- **Wooden board.** Find a board that fits into your dipping can for making wax sheets for rolled candles.
- **Glass meat baster.** A glass (not plastic) meat baster is handy for squirting wax into tight spaces.
- **Pillowcase.** For holding wax blocks while you break them into smaller pieces with a hammer.

CAUTION

Keep the lid for your large water pot handy as a fire safety device.

EASY MEASURING METHODS

To determine the weight of wax, simply weigh it on a scale. Almost all candlemaking paraffins are sold in 11-pound blocks. If you break one in quarters, you have four 2¾-pound blocks.

If you wish to determine the volume of solid wax, calculate by displacement. Partly fill a large measuring cup or other calibrated container with water, noting how much water you add. Carefully drop in the chunks of wax you wish to measure, making sure they are fully submerged. Subtract the starting volume of the water from the final level of water and wax to find the volume of the wax.

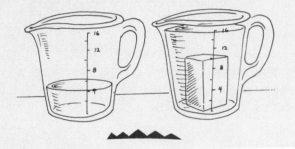

◆ **Ice pick, knitting needle, or wicking needle.** For making wick holes in hardened candles. Wicking needles look like oversized crewel embroidery needles. The hole in them is large enough to carry a wick and the needle itself is long enough so that the needle can be inserted in one end and grasped at the other and the wick pulled through.

◆ **Plastic bags.** For measuring mold volumes and storing unused, cooled wax.

◆ **Pliers.** To pull wicks through molds, hold a candle while it's being overdipped, and squeeze tabs around the end of a wick.

- ◆ **Ruler.** For measuring lengths of vessels, candles, and wick.
- ◆ **Screwdriver.** Necessary for screw-type wick-holder molds.
- ◆ **Liquid soap.** Perfect for lubricating rubber molds.
- ◆ **Knife.** Keep a butter knife handy. When it's heated, you can sculpt candles or adhere appliqués to their surface.
- ◆ **Propane torch.** Use to create odd surface effects and melt wax off surfaces. Be careful when using a torch on wax. Keep the flame as far away from a candle's surface as possible and be prepared to move quickly if the wax begins to burn. The flashpoint of most waxes is 440°F.
- ◆ **Heat pen or pointed metal tool.** A heat pen resembles a soldering iron or a woodburning tool. It is made with a tip that will heat up enough to melt designs into wax or help adhere decorations or appliqués. If you do not have access to a heat pen, use a pointed metal tool that can withstand heat.
- ◆ **Cardboard.** Small pieces for holding the wicks apart from each other while dipping candles.
- ◆ **Hooks or pegs.** For hanging just-dipped candles while they cool.
- ◆ **Moldmaking materials.** Such as silicone rubber, natural rubber, and sand (see chapter 8).

SAFETY EQUIPMENT AND PROCEDURES

The importance of safety in candlemaking cannot be overstated. You must be aware of this fact at all times: Making candles requires the use of flammable materials around heat sources. Avoid working around open flames unless it is absolutely necessary.

Always heat wax in a double boiler or in a heating vessel with encased elements. When using a double boiler, never let the water boil away! Replenish the water in a double boiler frequently to maintain the proper level.

If direct heating is called for in a candlemaking method, observe extreme caution during these steps!

Never leave burning candles unattended.

Keep the following things handy for extinguishing a fire, and know how to use them:

◆ Fire extinguisher (ABC type)
◆ Metal pan lid to starve a fire of oxygen
◆ Baking soda to smother flames
◆ A damp cloth or towel

If a fire starts while you are making candles, turn off the source of heat and use an extinguisher, pan lid, baking soda, or damp towel to deplete the oxygen level available to the fire and cause it to go out.

Never use water to extinguish a wax fire! This would cause wax to splatter and increase your chances of being burned.

Splattering on Skin

If you splatter yourself or even accidentally dip a finger into hot paraffin, it probably won't burn you severely, but it's wise to have cold water nearby so that you can submerge your skin until the wax is cool enough to remove. Paraffin will cool and chip off, but the stickiness of beeswax prevents chipping. The heat of the wax will continue to burn until the wax is removed or completely cooled. Continue to cool your skin for a minute or two after the wax is removed to limit the burn.

Pouring Wax Safely

When you are pouring wax, be sure you have a firm grip on the pouring vessel and a comfortable pouring angle. You need to pour smoothly. Don't be tempted to contort yourself in order to pour a perfect candle. You could be putting yourself at risk of spilling or dropping wax. Don't do it — no candle is worth burning yourself over!

Always keep rags and pot holders handy for gripping hot metal handles (and for wiping up wax and water spills).

CAUTION

If you do spill a large quantity of hot wax on yourself, cool water is the best remedy. If you think you've done real harm, call 911, but continue to keep the area cool — not cold or iced. An extreme temperature change is as much of a shock to your skin as the burn.

Never, Nevers

Never pour wax down the drain! It will solidify and cause you tremendous (and expensive) plumbing problems. Pour extra wax into cups or tins. After it's cooled, store the wax in plastic bags for reuse. You will be able to recycle all the wax you don't use up.

It's not a good idea to pour your double-boiler water down the drain, either. Although it is 99 percent water, it most likely contains some wax. You have two choices — either pour it outside, or allow it to cool thoroughly and remove the solid wax from the surface before pouring the water down the drain.

Candlemaking safety is a lot like cooking safety. Slow, intentional movement, knowing where you are moving from and to, and having a well-laid-out work area are the keys to safety.

A FEW WORDS ABOUT CLEANING UP

I am a firm believer in the notion that a clean workplace is a safer workplace. The less to trip over, spill on yourself, or move out of the way, the easier it is to function and focus on the job at hand rather than the obstacles.

I recommend you work on a covered surface so that wax will be caught on a disposable covering. If your candlemaking grows to the point that you have a surface just for candles, it's nice to have a smooth countertop that can be scraped clean of wax so you can save the wax for future projects.

Wax on Your Clothes

If you get wax on your clothes, you have a few options for cleanup. Try one of the following procedures.

- Wait until the wax cools; if it is sitting on the surface of the fibers, scrape it off.
- Put the cloth in the freezer and chip the wax off when it's most brittle.

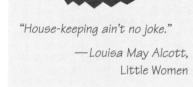

"House-keeping ain't no joke."

—*Louisa May Alcott,*
Little Women

- Place the cloth between layers of kraft paper and iron the wax out of the cloth and into the paper, changing the paper frequently to prevent the wax from redepositing onto the cloth.
- Boil the cloth in water, then wash and dry it. A caution here: When you pull the cloth out of the water, wax can be redeposited in a different place!
- Take the article of clothing to a dry cleaner, letting him know you have a wax stain. Dry-cleaning solvent dissolves wax but it's best for the cleaner to know about the wax so he can try spot cleaning first.

To clean your tools, molds, and containers, line your oven rack with aluminum foil, preheat to 150–170°F (do not exceed the temperature stated on your metal mold instructions, or you may melt the solder), and place all of your utensils upside down on the foil. The wax will run out onto the foil, and your tools will simply need a quick wipe with a clean cloth while they are still hot to complete the cleaning.

"It is better to light one candle than curse the darkness."

— motto of the
Christopher Society

CANDLE WAX REMOVER

Candle Wax Remover, a citrus-based product, is available through candle suppliers. This chemical will dissolve the thin film of wax that remains after you have wiped all of the hot liquid wax off a container or a surface. It can also be used if you are carving with wax or have created a molded candle with a small blemish and you want to smooth the surface.

For example, I use machinable wax (a hard, carvable wax) for designing models for homemade candle molds. When I am nearly finished, I use Candle Wax Remover to smooth the rough edges so that I will not transfer any blemishes onto the master mold and subsequently onto every candle I produce. To use the product, simply put some of the liquid onto a soft rag and lightly rub the rough areas. The liquid will slowly dissolve the roughness, but be careful — it may change the surface appearance of the wax.

CHAPTER 6
Rolled Candles and Sheet Wax

A BROOD FOUNDATION

Beeswax sheets originated as a tool for the beekeeper and are used, in natural color only, to line new hives. This gives the bees a foundation on which to build subsequent layers of comb. Beekeepers refer to these natural beeswax sheets as brood foundation.

Making candles from sheets of wax is the simplest method of candlemaking, provided you use purchased rolling sheets. These are readily available in dozens of colors and in two major types. Generally, commercially available wax sheets are made of pure beeswax, but if they are not clearly labeled as such, I recommend you ask. They may be paraffin or a beeswax/paraffin blend, and should be less expensive if this is the case.

The most common type is the honeycomb sheet. This sheet is usually 8 inches by 16 inches and embossed with a hexagonal honeycomb pattern. It is made by running flat sheets of beeswax under an embossing wheel. For candlemaking, dozens of colors are added to sheets that have been bleached. The other kind of rolling sheet is smooth-finished, without the honeycomb pattern. It can be used to roll candles and for a number of other projects in this chapter.

ROLLING METHODS

There are two basic ways to roll sheet wax. You can start at the narrow (8-inch) end of an 8- by 16-inch sheet to roll a cylindrical candle. Or cut

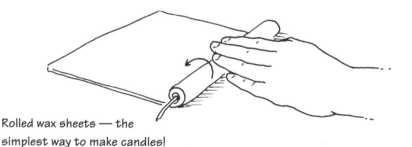

Rolled wax sheets — the simplest way to make candles!

an 8- by 16-inch sheet in half diagonally, using a metal straightedge with a knife or razor blade. Begin rolling at the 8-inch end, moving toward the point of the triangle you've created with the diagonal cut. Maintain the long, straight edge to create a flat candle bottom. This shape will make a spiral candle.

Rolled on the diagonal for a more decorative effect.

SIMPLE ROLLED CANDLES

Materials
- Commercial wax rolling sheets
- Wick (36- or 42-ply flat-braided wick for beeswax rolling sheets; 30-ply or 1/0 square braid for paraffin sheets)

Equipment
- Metal straightedge
- Scissors
- Sharp knife or razor blade
- Suitable cutting surface

1. Prepare a work surface. Be sure you have a mat or heavy board to cut on.
2. Cut your wick 2 inches longer than the length of the finished candle you wish to make.
3. Keep the sheets in a warm place for several hours before rolling or warm them with a blow-dryer or on cardboard placed on top of a heating pad. Check them every minute or so. It doesn't take long for a thin sheet of wax to melt. The wax sheets must be at room temperature or warmer in order to be flexible enough to roll without cracking.

"How far that little candle throws his beams! So shines a good deed in a naughty world."

—William Shakespeare, The Merchant of Venice

4. On the edge of a flat surface (like the edge of a table or countertop), bend a ⅛-inch fold into the end of the wax. This is the wick channel, so it must run parallel to the length (height) of your candle. Turn the wax over, so that the L-shaped channel is facing up. Center the wick in this channel: Press and bend the wax firmly around the wick.

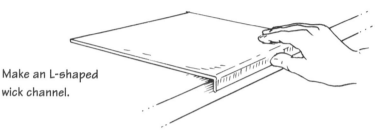

Make an L-shaped wick channel.

5. Carefully begin rolling the wax with a firm, even pressure so that you avoid leaving air bubbles between wax layers. Roll in a straight line so the bottom — and, for a cylindrical candle, the top as well — is even. When you get to the end of the wax, press it firmly to the previous layer. Then roll the entire candle on your work surface to make it as round as possible and to adhere the layers.

6. Trim the bottom wick flush with the wax, trimming the wax to make it flat, if necessary. Trim the top wick to ½ inch.

Finishing Touches

You may want to finish off your rolled candles on the top or bottom. Here are two possibilities.

Carving a Tapered Top. Taking care not to cut the wick, trim the wax tip into a cone shape with a sharp knife to make a tapered candle top.
Melting a Flat Bottom. Heat an old cookie sheet, pie tin, or cake pan on the stove. Hold the bottom of your rolled candle on the metal until it begins to melt and flatten. This technique will also prevent the candle from unrolling because it melts the layers together.

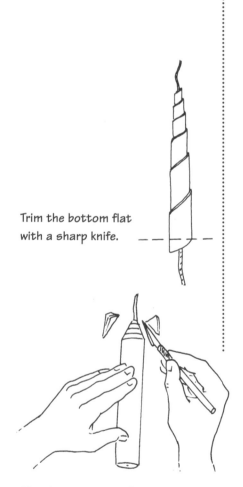

Trim the bottom flat with a sharp knife.

Give the top a taper by trimming it.

HOMEMADE SHEET WAX

*One pound (454 g) of wax makes approximately four sheets,
enough for four 10- by 1-inch candles.*

The wax and wick options specified in this recipe are meant to be only guidelines. The relationship among a wax's melting point, the selected wick type and size, and a finished candle's diameter is critical in determining the successful burning characteristics of a finished candle. Remember to take notes so that you can repeat your successes or make adjustments for your next batch of candles.

Materials
◆ One of following wax formulas:

Formula A
1 pound of beeswax

Formula B
½ pound (227 g) of beeswax and
½ pound (227 g) of paraffin with
a 130–150°F melting point

Formula C
1 pound (454 g) of paraffin and
2 tablespoons (30 ml) of stearic
acid (optional)

Formula D
3 parts paraffin to 1 part
microcrystalline, for pliability

Formula E
2 parts beeswax to 1 part paraffin

◆ Vegetable oil
◆ Color, as desired
◆ Scent, as desired

Equipment
◆ Double boiler or concealed-
element heater
◆ Kraft paper or foil
◆ Scale
◆ Thermometer

◆ Ladle
◆ Cookie sheet
◆ Cake pan and melting cans, if add-
ing more than one color or scent
◆ Aluminum foil
◆ Paper towel

SELECTING WICK SIZE
When choosing wicks for candles that increase in diameter from top to bottom, be aware that there is no single proper size. Any wick you choose could be too big to suit the smaller dimension of the top or too small to suit the larger dimension of the bottom. Your best bet is to choose a wick size that is suitable for the thicker parts of the candle and understand that the thinner top will burn quicker.

1. Cover a level work area with kraft paper or foil. Make sure you have everything you need within reach. Weigh your ingredients on the scale.

2. If you are using a double boiler, put the paraffin and beeswax or the paraffin and stearic acid into the melting pot and put it on a trivet in the water pot. Turn the heat to medium high. If you have a concealed-element heater, melt the waxes or paraffin/stearic acid directly in the pot. Keep the pot turned no higher than 180°F.

3. Line a cookie sheet with foil, keeping it as smooth as possible. With a little vegetable oil on a paper towel, wipe oil onto the foil.

4. When the wax reaches at least 150°F, but no higher than 180°F, you can add the colorant and scent if you're using them. If you want to make more than one color or scent, divide the wax into three or four 12-ounce cans, placed in a cake pan filled with water over low heat. Color or scent each one differently to make several different sheets. Stir well to dissolve and disperse the colors and scents.

5. Gripping the edge of the can of colored/scented wax or pouring from your wax-melting pot or ladling from your concealed-element heater, put enough wax on the foil-covered cookie sheet to make a wax tablet $\frac{1}{16}$ to $\frac{1}{8}$ inch thick. If your cookie sheet is not flat or your table is not level, you may need to tilt the cookie sheet a bit to make an even thickness of wax.

Pour hot wax into a foil-lined tray to make wax sheets.

6. When the wax is congealed and cool to the touch, remove the wax and foil from the cookie sheet and turn it over so the foil is facing up. Carefully peel the foil off the wax sheet.

Turn over wax and foil to peel the foil from the wax.

Dip wet plywood into wax to make wax sheets.

7. At this point, the sheet is still pliable and can be rolled following the preceding directions for rolled candles. You may trim the sheet's edges before rolling since the sheets are usually thinner at the edges. Or you can roll your candles first and trim them after.

Alternative Method for Making Sheet Wax

If you have a relatively deep and large-mouthed melting pot, you can try this method. Soak a piece of plywood in water for at least 1 hour to prevent it from absorbing hot wax. Dip the plywood into hot wax, then cool for 1 minute. Repeat this five times. When the wax is cooled, scrape it off the edges of the plywood, then remove the sheets from both sides of the wood.

You can make these sheets thicker than five layers if you want. You can make multicolored layers, too.

Trim the wax from the edges of the plywood, then remove the wax sheet.

Playing with Wax Sheets

It's fun to play with homemade sheet wax when it's still very warm because you can sculpt it as you roll. If it becomes too cool to shape, drop the wax into 100–110°F water to resoften it and knead to proper consistency. Here are a few ideas for techniques to try.

◆ Cut your wick extra long, roll a candle, then keep on rolling the warm wax into a thinner, longer taper.

◆ Roll several tapers (described above) and twist together. Or squeeze the tapers into odd shapes!

◆ Overdip (page 118) the candles to resoften them, and play some more.

◆ Pour thicker sheets and roll votive or pillar shapes.

The more you work with wax, the more you'll discover its amazingly tactile nature. Most people don't think of hot wax as a sculpting medium, but when it's between the liquid and solid states, it's very enjoyable and messy to play with.

VOTIVES OF A DIFFERENT HUE

Pour or dip individual sheets of wax in different colors using one of the sheet-wax formulas. Once the sheets are cool enough to work, roll the layers together around an extra-long wick to make a multi-colored log. While the roll is still warm, slice the log into pillars or votives. After you cut the first pillar or votive from the roll, pull the wick up through the center until it's approximately 1/2 inch above the top surface of the wax. Continue pulling the wick through the remaining roll so each candle you cut will have wick extending from its top. The roll must be warm for the wick to slide through.

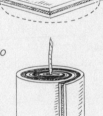

Cleaning Up

Cleanup is critical to your next candlemaking session. If you tidy up well, you won't have to start your next session with a cleanup.

1. First, decide whether you want to save the waxes you've made as separate colors or blend them all into one muddy color that you can dilute later. If you're blending together, pour all the leftover wax into a cake pan; to keep colors separate, pour into cupcake tins.

2. Allow to cool, then pop the wax out and into plastic bags that you label with the wax and color combinations, such as "paraffin/beeswax 50/50 blue/red/yellow." You may not be able to remember the color(s) or the wax content the next time you use it, so labeling is important.

3. Using rags or paper towels, wipe out anything that contained wax before it solidifies.

4. Locate all of your tools, such as knives, scissors, and rulers; scrape the wax off them; and put them back where they belong.

5. After all the waxy containers have been emptied, wad up the paper you used to cover your work area. If you spilled, you can peel the wax off the paper before you throw it away and save it for later use.

6. Pour any leftover hot water outside or let it cool, remove the wax on the surface, and pour the water down the drain. Never pour wax down the drain!

Wax and oils have been poured and burned in containers since the earliest oil lamps. Molded candles have been made since the fifteenth century with molds made of wood. While the wooden molds solved some candlemaking problems, they were a headache when used with beeswax because it is so sticky. So even then, attempts were being made to find better mold materials. Luckily for us, many effective materials are now available, and releasing candles from their forms is not as much of a chore.

Some molds, like those used for gelatin, are found in every kitchen or garage sale. Other molds are high-tech. Some are disposable, like milk cartons and tin cans. Others will last through hundreds of pours. In any event, all molds work on the same basic principle: They create a wax-tight cavity threaded with a centered wick in which to pour wax to create a candle that is shaped like the mold and will pull away from the mold material easily.

As a category, poured candles cover a broad spectrum of types including container, molded, and cast candles. To produce any of these candles, wax is shaped by pouring it into a form. Among the simplest poured candles are those we call container candles.

CONTAINER CANDLES

Unless you have access to special container waxes that have a high oil content and can burn with very little oxygen, I recommend that you pour into containers 5 inches or less in depth. If a container is deeper than that, your candle may put itself out as it burns down. Following are a few additional guidelines in selecting a container.

- Use widemouthed containers, not ones that taper at the neck.
- Ceramic and metal are also suitable container materials. In this case, you will be pouring one color, since you will not be able to see any of the wax except the top surface.
- Stay away from wood or any other flammable containers. If you want to have an outer wooden container, use the wood as a holder for a concealed glass or ceramic container. This is much safer, and the candle is easier to replace when it burns down.
- If you use glass, choose relatively sturdy glasses, not delicate ones. A plain glass container can be a beautiful beginning for a very ornately poured, multicolored candle. A fancy glass, such as cut crystal or bubbly, blown, swirling-colors glass will probably look better with a single color of wax burning in it, to allow the beauty of the glass to glow on its own.

You can make poured candles in plain or decorative containers.

SCENTS AND SOOT

Poorly formulated container candles cause more indoor air problems than do other types of candles. Container candles require softer (low-melting-point) waxes in order to burn inside an oxygen-deprived environment. Waxes designed for this purpose are formulated to offer the proper burning characteristics.

You have to be careful when adding scent to these low-melting-point waxes, because you are further softening the wax by adding oil. Burning soft-wax candles with high percentages of scent will produce smoke and spew soot into your home. Although you may be tempted to add more than the recommended amount of scent, I caution you against doing so. Instead, find a stronger scent or use an additive that will enable the wax to accept a higher percentage of scent without impacting its melting point.

For more information on this, please read the sections on additives, scenting candles, and indoor air quality.

Wax manufacturers have developed new one-pour container waxes to reduce shrinkage and adhere better to the container walls. They enable the candlemaker to simply melt and pour the wax, insert the wick, and allow it to cool — no second pour, no muss, no fuss!

You can find one-pour waxes through candlemaking suppliers. However, because they are custom blends, using additives can be unpredictable and is not recommended. Wax manufacturers tell me that home candlemakers cause more problems using additives in these specially blended waxes.

Use these products straight and see what happens. Work on finding the proper wick to suit the wax before you introduce additives. Then, if you still feel a need to add synthetic waxes or microcrystallines to achieve a particular end, add them one at a time, testing the results by burning the candle after each try, so that you can pinpoint whether you are introducing a problem into your recipe.

CONTAINER CANDLE

The wax and wick specified in this recipe are meant as guidelines. The relationship among a wax's melting point, the selected wick type and size, and a finished candle's diameter are critical in determining the successful burning characteristics of a finished candle. The size of wick depends on the size of the container and the wax in the candle. Remember to take notes so that you can repeat your successes or to make adjustments for your next batch of candles.

Materials
- Wax (paraffin with a low melting point, 125–130°F)
- Wick (cored wick is preferable, but noncored wick will work; medium-sized wick with a paper, cotton, or zinc core is recommended)
- Wick tab(s) for each container
- Color, as desired
- Scent, as desired

Equipment
- Double boiler or concealed-element heater
- Thermometer
- Ladle and/or pouring pitcher
- Dowel, and small weights for suspending wick if using the noncored variety
- Cake pan and several tin cans if you plan to use multiple colors
- Skewer, chopstick, dowel, or other small poker
- Containers

1. To determine approximately how much wax you need to make your container candles, pour water into your vessels or into a plastic bag inserted into your container if you want to keep it dry right before pouring wax into it. Either measure that amount of water in a measuring cup or pour it into your marked melting pot to see which line it comes up to.

2. Place determined quantity of wax in melting pot or concealed-element heater setup and begin melting it.

3. Attach a wick tab to a length of wick at least 1 inch longer than the height of your container. Trim any excess wick from the bottom of the tab so it will sit flat on the bottom of your container. If you're using uncored wick, weight one end of the wick instead of tabbing it. Suspend the other end of the wick from a dowel hung across the opening of the container.

4. Since wax shrinks as it cools and will shrink more if it is poured into a cold container, warm your containers in one of the following ways:

◆ Place in a 150°F oven for a few minutes.
◆ Run under hot water.
◆ Put a cake pan full of water on the stove on medium heat and place the containers in the pan to warm them.

Caution: If your containers are glass, warm them slowly and not above 150°F.

5. When the wax reaches 150–160°F, it is ready to pour. If you plan to use several colors of wax, divide the melted wax among several tin cans and add color and/or scent to it. Stir well to disperse.

6. To begin, pour about ½ inch of wax into the container. Immediately center the wick or wick tab in the bottom of the container, and if necessary hold it until it stays put. This is called the tack pour. Let the wax cool slightly to hold the wick in place.

7. If you're pouring one color only, fill the container to within ½ inch of the top and allow the wax to begin to congeal. When about ⅛ inch of wax has hardened on the surface, break the surface with a poker and make several holes around the wick toward the bottom of the container. Pour a small amount of wax into these holes.

½"

The tack pour holds the wick in place (step 6).

WICK HOLDERS FOR CONTAINER CANDLES

Weighting the wick and tying it to a dowel is the least technological way of centering a wick inside a container or mold. New developments to aid the candlemaker in this endeavor help stabilize both the top and the bottom of the wick. For instance, double-sided sticky tabs adhere to the inside of the container and hold the wick tab tightly, which prevents it from moving or floating during pouring.

In addition, you can purchase a wick holder. This product is made of a piece of sheet metal that sits across the top of your container and has a tapered opening, allowing you to thread the wick through a hole and catch it in the narrow tapered slit in the metal. The metal holds the wick steady and centered while you pour wax along the sides of the metal anchor. This system works well for any type of wick, but it is especially helpful for cored wick, which may move during the pouring process but cannot be knotted around a dowel.

This second pour, or repour, is called the cap pour. It removes air bubbles and fills in the center depression of the candle as the wax shrinks. If you did not repour at all, there's a good chance your cooled candle would develop a deep conical hole in the center because wax tends to shrink away from the wick toward the sides of the container as it cools. The repouring process also fills in subsurface cavities.

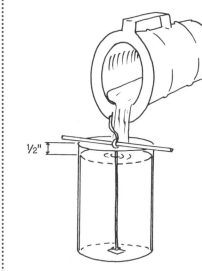

Fill the container to within ½ inch of the top (step 7).

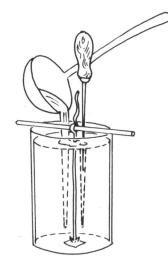

Pierce the surface and pour the wax cap to fill in any air holes (step 7).

8. Repeat the repouring process several times until all the wax is cool.
9. When the candle is cooled, trim the wick to ½ inch above the surface of the wax.

Yipes! Stripes!

If you want more than one color in your container candles, you can achieve this effect in several ways. Divide your melted wax and color it. In the container, pour a stripe as wide as you like, then wait until it has cooled enough to have at least a ⅛-inch solid surface before you repour. If you want very distinct stripes, wait until the layer is even harder because the hot wax of the second pour will tend to melt into the first color and blend with it. Repeat this process until you have all the colored stripes you desire.

For a different kind of striping effect, wait until the wax of one layer of color is cooled to at least a ⅛-inch thickness. Then slide your poker down the outer edge of the congealed wax to create channels for the next color to fill up. This makes vertical or diagonal stripes against the horizontal poured stripes.

Or you can push your poker into the wax along the sides of the glass container to create different geometric shapes or to give an illusion of mountains or water. These will be highlighted when you pour the next color. This is worth experimenting with!

When the last color of your multicolored container candle is poured and slightly solidified, poke through the surface as far down as you can along the wick to remove air bubbles and repour the last color to fill in the hole. Repeat this as the candle cools to prevent a conical hole from forming in your container.

When the candle has cooled completely, trim the wick to ½ inch above the top surface.

GETTING HUNG UP

The ideal container candle will burn by completely liquefying the surface of the wax and exhausting it without creating a pool that drowns the wick. Wax left on the side of the jar, called hang-up, indicates that the wick is too small or the melting point of the wax is too high to be melted by the wick used.

wax
hang-up

GEL CANDLES

Candle gel is a stiffened gel that must be scooped or cut into pieces small enough to fit into your melting container. It comes from the manufacturer in 360-pound (55-gallon) barrels but may be sold to home candlemakers in chunks by weight. It may also be melted by your candle supplier and poured into smaller buckets for retail sale.

Selecting Containers

Generally, the containers used for candle gel are clear, so that Versagel's unique transparency is visible. Many people use the high polymer grade (HP), which allows them to suspend glitter or small, nonflammable objects along the outer walls of the candles, creating an effect similar to that of an aquarium or a terrarium. As with all container candles, select wide-mouthed vessels, so that the flame has sufficient oxygen for good combustion.

Making Gel Candles

Melt the gel to at least 200°F (up to 221°F maximum) using a concealed-element heater with elements that surround the bottom and sides of the container. It takes considerably more time to melt gel than regular wax — up to an hour or longer. (Large-scale manufacturers who use the gel straight from the 55-gallon drum heat it using heat belts that strap around the drum; this can take up to 24 hours to melt the gel.) I had no luck at all melting it in a double boiler. The water simply cannot transmit enough heat through the double-boiler vessel to heat this material; it requires direct heat.

Choosing The Wick

Select a wick that is one size larger than what you would use for an equivalent sized wax-filled container candle. In some cases, a metal-cored (zinc) wick may be necessary to achieve the proper wick-to-gel ratio. Some suppliers sell a new product called Gelwick, which is designed specifically to use with candle gel. It is a zinc-cored wick that produces a small flame and is designed to create a 2.5-inch wax pool. Gel candles with larger diameters may require multiple wicks.

Gel candles are also a good candidate for adhesive wick stickers placed on the inside of your container, a high-collar wick tab, and a sturdy metal wick holder on top of the container; these prevent the hot gel from drooping the wick while you pour. Inserting the wick after you pour may produce bubbles around the wick, but these can be removed after the candle cools (see below). Always use a metal wick tab to hold the wick in place: As the candle burns, the pool of liquid gel may not be viscous enough to hold the wick steady.

Coloring Agents

Because you cannot add paraffin or other candlemaking additives to gel, liquid dyes must be used. Do not use color chips or blocks, as their wax base will cause the gel to lose its transparency and suspend the color particles in the gel without truly coloring the gel itself. Suppliers who sell candle gel generally stock the necessary wick, dyes, and scents to help you get started with this product.

Scents

Since gel burns so hot and so slowly, Penreco recommends using fragrances with flash points above 170°F. For best results you must use fragrances specifically formulated for candlemaking rather than essential oils. You must also select scents with good hydrocarbon solubility, as some scents are more soluble in mineral oil than others. To check whether the scent you are using will blend into gel, test your fragrance in pure mineral oil. First, use one drop of scent to three drops of oil (25:75 ratio).

If this mixture appears to become a perfectly blended liquid, do a second test using three drops of fragrance to one drop of mineral oil (75:25 ratio). The scent should be completely soluble and not separate (polarize) from the oil.

Once your tests have shown that the scent will dissolve in mineral oil, you are ready to heat the gel to 203 to 221°F, then blend in the dye and fragrances. Stir well to completely incorporate the color and scent. When the temperature is between 185 and 203°F, pour the gel into the container.

Candle Gel and Bubbles

Candle gel is transparent, so bubbles show. Bubbles naturally rise to the top and pop as the mixture heats up and becomes less viscous. Bubbles can also be deliberately introduced into your design by agitating the viscous material or by pouring it quickly from high above the container. The gel begins to solidify as soon as it leaves the heat source, and the simple act of pouring can reintroduce air, trapping bubbles in the gel, as it flows out of the melting vessel and into the container. Most people consider the bubbles a natural part of the gel candle and include them as a normal part of their design. If you do not want any bubbles in your candle, you will have to play with techniques to see what works best for you.

Reducing Bubbles

- ◆ You can heat the gel to the high point (221°F) to completely eliminate bubbles, and then pour very slowly and close to the container so that you do not introduce new bubbles as you pour.
- ◆ It may be helpful to preheat your glass container, so that you are not pouring hot gel into a cold container and causing it to cool too quickly, which forms bubbles.
- ◆ Some people allow the gel to cool to the pouring low point (185°F) and pour slowly.

- If you are using the Versagel HP grade and wish to suspend items (including shells, glass, or chunks of colored Versagel), carefully submerge and situate them before the gel cools much below 170°F, when it will begin to stiffen quickly into its gel structure. This process may reintroduce bubbles, which can be removed by reheating the cooled container candle in an oven at a temperature of 131 to 158°F. However, it is best not to do this in your home oven but in an oven reserved only for craft use.
- If you use a thick-walled container, you can also achieve the same result — eliminating bubbles with heat — by heating the container with a blow dryer to force the bubbles upward. However, if the walls of the container are too thin, the glass will break from the heat.

Layering Colors and Creating Designs

Because this is a one-pour product with no shrinkage, you can safely pour one color, wait until it cools, and then pour a second color without risking that shrinkage will cause the second color to ooze over the edges of the first color. If you want to strategically place objects along the outer edges of the container, pour some gel into the container, swirl the liquid around to coat the sides of the container, and then set the objects into the gel and allow them to cool in place. Then pour the inner layer of gel to fill the center of the candle container. This technique can also be used to create an outer layer with metallic glitter particles suspended in it while the center is filled with clear gel.

Candle gel is a product with many possibilities, but it requires different handling than traditional candlemaking wax and should not be combined with other candlemaking ingredients, as it is incompatible with wax. Unlike wax, spilled Versagel simply peels off smooth surfaces but, because of its elastic nature, it cannot be ironed out of fabric. Be sure to wear an apron!

Containers of a Different Kind

The possibilities for container candles are as infinite as the containers you find. The worst that can happen is making a candle that doesn't burn well. If that happens, simply put the container in a cake pan of hot water on the stove and melt the wax back out of the container for reuse. Here are a few ideas you might want to try.

Outdoor Citronella Candle. Use a cinder block or decorative cement block as a container. Make wax scented with citronella essential oil. Embed the cinder block in wet sand, which will act as a temporary base when you pour the wax. You can use several wicks — cored zinc wick is the best, or try primed, all-cotton shoelaces. Tab them, suspend them from a dowel, or simply embed them in the sand, making sure they extend above the cement surface since you will probably have to hold them up in the centered position as the wax cools.

Pour in about ½ inch of wax and allow it to partially cool, in order to create a base so less wax will seep into the sand. Then pour the rest of the way, and poke and repour as indicated for the container candle until the wax has cooled.

Sit this candle on a same-sized piece of wood on your porch or deck or backyard all year round. When lit, it will repel insects. When not in use, it can act as a plant stand, door stop, or part of a rock wall!

Shell Candles. Walnut shells or seashells can be filled with wax and tiny cored wicks inserted as it cools. These can be floated in a punch bowl or across a pond at twilight.

Orange Peel Candles. Carefully peel off orange peel in hemispheres. Pour wax into these natural containers with or without adding additional scent, and insert cored wicks as the wax cools. These are great table decorations at a barbecue.

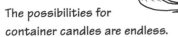

The possibilities for container candles are endless.

MOLDED CANDLES

It is possible to make candles of almost any shape using a mold. But the more complex the shape, the more complex the mold must be. Molds can be disposable, meaning that you can tear or cut the mold away from the candle. They can be one-piece molds, designed to slide off the candle. Or they can be multipart molds, which have a seam, or parting line, engineered to divide a candle along a plane. This allows you to pull the mold off without breaking the candle's shape.

Understanding Draft and Undercut

Draft is a slight taper in a mold that makes the open end larger than the closed end so that a form created by the mold will tend to pop out easily. Draft is built into so many designs, such as yogurt and cottage cheese containers, we often don't notice it. It is possible to make a completely cylindrical candle in a mold without draft because wax shrinks slightly as it cools and lets the candle slide out. But with any more complex shape than a cylinder, draft is essential for using a one-piece mold.

Draft allows a one-piece mold to release the hardened candle.

Think of undercutting this way: It's any part of a shape that would prevent it from sliding out of a mold without bending or breaking off. Shapes with undercuts have to be made in molds of two pieces or more. The molds split in certain places called parting lines so they can be pulled off without breaking the candle. When you start looking at candle molds, you will find that more elaborate designs are usually made from two-piece molds.

The exceptions to this undercutting rule are molds made of soft silicone rubber. These are so flexible that they can be peeled off a candle like a glove, or so spongy that they compress as you pull a cooled candle out of them.

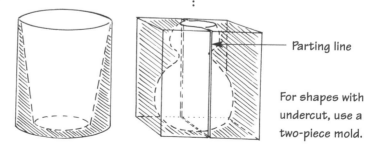

Parting line

For shapes with undercut, use a two-piece mold.

Disposable Molds

Disposable molds include items such as waxed milk cartons, yogurt containers, juice cans, and other found objects. These molds may require reinforcement with masking tape or may need to be poured at a low temperature so they don't melt. The only way to tell for sure is through experimentation.

If you use a tin can as a mold, the raised rings around the can may act as undercuts and make it difficult for you to remove a candle. You'll have to try it and see.

Wicking a Mold

Following are general wicking directions for common molds. You should consult the instructions that accompany commercial molds for further details.

If you're using a one-piece metal, acrylic, or rubber mold, it comes with a hole in the base through which you thread a wick, then hold it taut with wick sealer and a screw. Pull the wick up to the open end of the mold and tie it to a rod to keep it taut.

If you're using a two-piece plastic mold, tape the wick to one end of half the mold, pull it tightly across the shape, and tape it to the other end. Line up the two sides and slip them into the purchased mold holder to seal them together.

CAUTION

If you're using a natural rubber mold, do not use stearic acid. It will create pockmarks in the mold. If you want to harden the wax without using stearic acid, use 1 to 3 percent hardening microcrystalline or polymer.

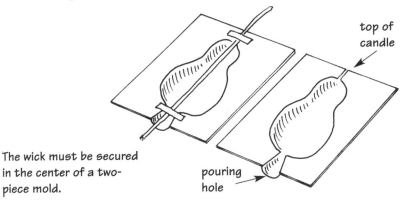

top of candle

The wick must be secured in the center of a two-piece mold.

pouring hole

If you're using a disposable mold, you have several options for wicking it:

♦ Thread a wick through a hole made in the bottom of the mold. Seal around the hole with putty, masking tape, chewing gum, or modeling clay. This is the preferred wicking method, since the bottom of the mold will become the top of the candle, giving the top of the candle a smooth, regular surface. The poured end of the candle will always have some irregularities from the pouring process.

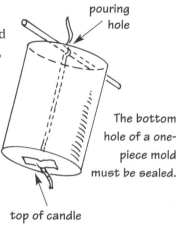

pouring hole

The bottom hole of a one-piece mold must be sealed.

top of candle

♦ Pour the wax and allow it to cool, then pierce a wick hole in the center of the candle with a hot ice pick or knitting needle. You will have to use primed wick in order to push it down through the hole. This can be difficult to do, but this is the best way to wick reusable containers like gelatin molds if you don't want to poke holes in the bottoms of them.

♦ Suspend a wick from a stick laid across the top of the mold, using a metal washer to weight the bottom end.

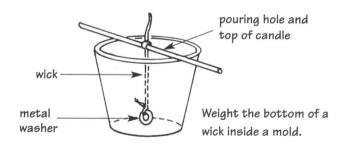

pouring hole and top of candle

wick

metal washer

Weight the bottom of a wick inside a mold.

MOLDED CANDLES

The wax and wick specified in this recipe are guidelines. The relationship among a wax's melting point, the selected wick type and size, and a finished candle's diameter are critical in determining the successful burning characteristics of a finished candle. Remember to take notes so that you can repeat your successes or make adjustments for your next batch of candles.

Materials

◆ Wax (paraffin with a medium melting point of 135–145°F)
◆ Beeswax, optional, up to 50 percent of the weight of the paraffin
◆ Stearic acid, 10 percent of the weight of the paraffin
◆ Wick (1/0 square braid for a candle 2 to 3 inches in diameter. Other sizes determined by the diameter of the mold and the wax content. If you are using 50 percent or more beeswax, increase wick size one or more sizes.)
◆ Color, as desired
◆ Scent, as desired

Equipment

◆ Double boiler or concealed-element heater
◆ Thermometer
◆ Pitcher or ladle
◆ Skewer, chopstick, or dowel
◆ Masking tape
◆ Ice pick or knitting needle
◆ Mold
◆ Mold release or vegetable oil
◆ Bucket
◆ Weight, such as a brick or a heavy piece of metal
◆ Razor blade or sharp knife
◆ Nylon panty hose

1. Determine the volume of your mold, using the method described for Container Candles (see page 78), or melt the amount recommended by the mold supplier for your particular mold.

ADDING BEESWAX

The addition of beeswax to candle formulas increases a candle's burn time and the pliability of the wax. It also increases the possibility of wax sticking to a mold, so be sure to use mold release!

A COOLING BATH

Most molded candles naturally shrink from the mold's walls as they cool. This takes many hours but can be sped up slightly by water cooling. To do this properly, you need to be sure your bucket is the right size to hold the mold and the water needed to surround it.

Because the mold will displace water when you put it into the bucket, determine the proper water depth by holding the empty mold in the bucket while you fill it with water within ½ inch of the top of your mold. That way, you'll be all set when you need to transfer your freshly poured candle to its cooling water bath. It is difficult to add water to a bucket that's holding a mold filled with wax, and too much water would overflow into your wax and ruin your candle.

2. Melt the wax in the double boiler over medium-high heat or in a concealed-element heater. Add stearic acid and color/scent when wax is melted. Maintain the wax at 160–180°F by adjusting the heat, if necessary.

3. If there is any water in the mold, dry it out. Apply mold release or vegetable oil. Remember to apply vegetable oil sparingly so that the surface of your candle will not be mottled. If you're using a silicone rubber or RTV (room temperature vulcanizing) mold, you need to use little or no mold release or vegetable oil because they have a natural tendency to release from wax. When you touch the inside of one of these molds, it has an oily feel to it. If you are using a disposable mold, you can choose not to use mold release, since you can cut and peel the mold off the candle rather than having to release the candle from the mold.

4. Wick your mold (see page 88).

5. Prepare a water bath with cool (not cold) water, having determined the proper water depth before wicking the mold. If you're using a disposable mold, it may help to pour about ½ inch of wax in and allow it to begin to solidify before proceeding to fill the mold. This will serve two purposes — first, it will seal the handmade wick hole and prevent leakage, and, second, it will reduce the possibility of melting the mold.

6. When the wax has reached 160–180°F or the temperature required for your mold (consult the mold supplier's instructions — plastic molds require cooler temperatures), pour the wax into the mold slowly, pouring at a slant down the side of the mold, if possible, to prevent air bubbles.

7. Carefully transfer the filled mold into the water bath, weighting it down with a brick or other heavy weight to prevent the mold from floating up. The surface finish of your candle will be consistent only if the entire candle is submerged in water.

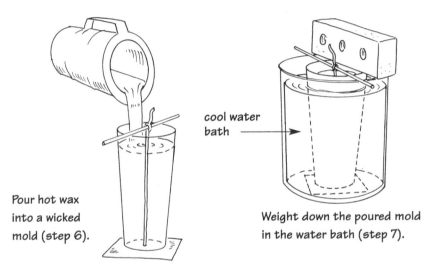

Pour hot wax into a wicked mold (step 6).

cool water bath

Weight down the poured mold in the water bath (step 7).

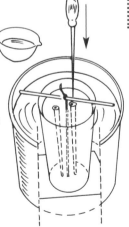

Pierce and pour more wax into the mold as it cools (step 8).

8. When a ⅛-inch-thick surface has formed on the wax, pierce a circle of holes around the wick, pushing down the length of the candle to release any air bubbles. Repour into the holes, being careful not to flow over the surface and down between the mold and the first pour. This would make releasing the candle very difficult.

9. Repeat this process several more times as you see the wax congealing and beginning to shrink. Leave the mold in the water for at least 1 hour.

10. Most candlemakers recommend that you wait at least 8 hours before trying to remove a candle from its mold. The candle must be completely cold to the touch before you remove it or you risk distorting it. If you see that the candle has released from the sides of the mold, it is probably ready to remove. Carefully turn the mold upside down and release the wick sealer. Remove the candle. If you have used a disposable mold, simply tear it off the candle.

11. If there are any seam lines in your candle, either from using a two-part mold or from a seam in a one-piece mold, carefully shave them off with a sharp razor blade or knife. Polish the candle with a piece of nylon panty hose to blend the carved area into the rest of the surface texture.

It's Stuck!

If, after a candle is completely cold, you cannot release it from the mold, try the following methods:

◆ Put it in the refrigerator for 30 minutes and try releasing it again.
◆ Run the mold under hot water. This will release the candle but will ruin the shiny surface you so carefully created by using the water bath. Don't despair — you can polish the surface using a piece of old panty hose or overdip the candle (page 118) and submerge it in cool water immediately.

Creative Effects with Molds

There are literally hundreds of different molds available on the market, from reproductions of antique European wooden molds, to tin and pewter taper molds from Colonial Williamsburg, to silicone molds of your favorite cartoon characters.

Since I like to embellish and experiment, I prefer to use simpler mold shapes so I can add my own variations to them. Following are a few of my favorite effects.

Multicolored Candles. Pour layers of different colors, either allowing the wax to cool between pours for sharp edges or allowing the colors to blend by pouring while the previous layer is still warm. You can also tilt the mold as you pour and cool successive layers to make a layered candle with angled wedges of color.

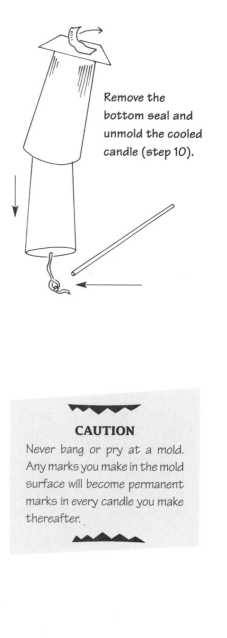

Remove the bottom seal and unmold the cooled candle (step 10).

CAUTION
Never bang or pry at a mold. Any marks you make in the mold surface will become permanent marks in every candle you make thereafter.

Chunk Candle. Pour chunks of wax, in one or many colors, by filling the compartments of heavy plastic ice cube trays with the same or several colors. Or pour a cake pan full of colored wax, then chop it into chunks.

Wick a mold and fill it with chunks. Pour clear melted wax or wax of a different color over and around the chunks. Tap the candle vigorously to ensure that air pockets between the chunks fill with wax.

The closer the chunks are to the outer surface, the more they will show through the poured wax. Contrasting the chunk colors against the poured color works well.

Chunk Candle with Objects. You can also use wax chunks to hold objects in place along the surface of a candle mold. Put flowers or seashells in along the mold wall, with chunks of wax to push them outward. Pour wax into the mold, and you will have a candle with a surface of flowers or shells.

In this case, you may want to pour wax of the same color as your chunks so the chunks will disappear into the solid color but your decorations won't. This technique works best with a large-diameter candle. If you choose to use this technique on a small-diameter candle, be aware that the objects on the surface may become loose as the candle burns. You may need to carve the outer surface to uncover the shells or trinkets, if wax has seeped around them. Use a knife or the curve of a spoon to shave the wax off. You can also use a propane torch to melt surface wax and expose your objects or contrasting colors.

Layered Candles. To layer colors from the outside in, begin by pouring wax into the mold. For this first, outermost pour it's usual to use a lighter color wax than for the inner layers.

When the wax has congealed to a thickness of ⅛ inch, carve off the top surface and pour the liquid wax in the center back out into your melting pot, leaving a ⅛-inch-thick layer around the inside of the mold. Now, pour a second, different color of wax into the center.

Pour out the liquid wax when the cooled layer is ⅛ inch thick.

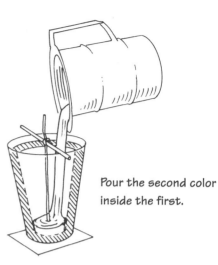

Pour the second color inside the first.

The inner color will show through the outer color, even more so when the candle is burning down and the flame illuminates one color against the other. You can also carve into the outer color to reveal the inner one using a heat pen or a carving tool heated over a flame.

Floating Candles. Use tart, candy, or soap molds to make floating candles. Most tart molds have lots of draft since they have been designed to allow you to release tarts easily. Use mold release or vegetable oil to ensure that the wax will come out of the molds.

Pour the wax and insert a cored wick as soon as there is a ¹⁄₁₆-inch film on the top. There will be a ¹⁄₁₆-inch film on the bottom as well, into which you can push the wick.

Floating candles are easy-to-make novelties.

FLOATING CANDLES

Floating candles have a tendency to migrate toward the edges of your punchbowl. To thwart this you can purchase gelling crystals, which thicken the water by gelling it. This enables you to place the candles into the liquid and expect them to stay put.

Gelling crystals are said to absorb up to 400 times their weight in water, as they expand to form large, gelled particles that are translucent like water but thick like gelatin. One teaspoon gels two to three cups of water. If a perfectly composed bowl of floating candles is what you desire, this product is for you!

ICE CANDLES

Many people's first experience with candlemaking was creating ice candles. This is a great project to do with children who are old enough to handle wax, and a chance to use up the ends of old candles. Just melt them down and filter out stray pieces of wick before pouring the candle.

Materials
- 1 empty, clean, waxed milk carton
- Masking tape
- Wax (medium-melting-point paraffin or recycled)
- 1 taper candle as tall as the milk carton
- Crushed ice

Equipment
- Double boiler or concealed-element heater
- Pouring can or metal pitcher

1. Reinforce the bottom and sides of the milk carton with masking tape.
2. Melt the paraffin or the recycled wax to 140°F in the double boiler or heater.
3. Center the taper candle in the milk carton and surround it with enough crushed ice to keep it upright. The more ice you use, the more lacy holes you'll have in the finished candle.
4. Slowly pour the wax into the milk carton. Fill it to the top. It's a good idea to place the container in a bin or bucket before pouring wax because water may start oozing from the carton as the hot wax melts the ice. Do not perform this step in your sink.
5. If the wax level appears to be dropping, refill it.
6. Wait at least 30 minutes. If the milk carton feels cool, peel it off the candle. Be sure to do this step over the sink because all the melted ice will pour out as you peel.

When you light this candle, it will really be the taper that's burning. You can replace the taper with another after the first one burns down.

Although you can make these candles with a primed wick suspended in the crushed ice, they never burn evenly or very well.

These are but a few of the possibilities you can create with molds. The variety increases yet again as we proceed into the realm of making our own molds and casts in the next chapter!

Casting a candle means you use a temporary form such as sand, balloons, or foil as the wax-holder. These molds last for only one use but are very inexpensive and allow for lots of personal flair.

Moldmaking, on the other hand, is an art unto itself and the result is a candlemaking form that can be reused. In this chapter, I will describe the basic principles of casting candles and making molds, some of the available materials for these techniques, and their advantages and disadvantages.

Cast candles are a great opportunity to exploit wax's plasticity. Whatever shape you can make for a cast candle, the wax will hold it. You can line a container with aluminum foil or a heavy plastic bag and pour a candle. You can also use foil in a free-form shape in sand. The possibilities are as endless as your imagination.

WICKS FOR SIMPLE CAST SHAPES

Because of their often free-form nature, cast candles may not always lend themselves to your preferred wicking method for making other types of candles. For cast candles, the wicking methods that work are:

◆ Inserting a cored wick when the wax is partially solidified
◆ Suspending a wick from a dowel extended across the rim of the vessel
◆ Boring a hole in the cooled candle with a heated ice pick or knitting needle, then inserting a cored wick

SAND CANDLES

In true sand cast candles, the sand becomes an integral part of the finished piece. In order for the sand and wax to form a sturdy crust on the outside of the candle, the wax must be very hot. Use wax with a melting point of at least 145°F.

Because the wax must be very hot for this project, I recommend you heat the wax directly on the stove without the water bath of the double-boiler system, or in a concealed-element heater. Alternatively, you can do this project at the beach over a campfire.

Materials
- Beach sand or commercially purchased potting sand (for special effects, try fancy colored sand)
- Wick (cored or primed)
- Wax with a high melting point
- Color, as desired
- Scent, as desired
- Water

Equipment
- Large pail or container (2-gallon or more capacity)
- Melting pot
- Direct heating element
- Thermometer
- Spoon
- Skewer, dowel, or other poking implement

1. To make the casting shape, fill the pail or other large container with the sand.

2. Add water to the sand until a handful, squeezed, holds its shape but is not muddy. Compact it well. The success of your casting depends on three things: the wax temperature, the wetness of the sand, and the compactness of the sand.

CAUTION

Do not leave the wax unattended when you are heating it directly on a stove or over a campfire. Monitor the temperature carefully. Wax is a fuel. It is very flammable, and should be treated with extreme care. Have baking soda, a damp cloth, a pot lid, and a fire extinguisher handy when you heat wax.

Press any shape into wet sand (step 3).

3. Dig out the desired shape for your candle or compress a shape, using your hand, a jar, or the handle of a tool. If you want the candle to have legs, a common 1970s sight, poke three deeper shapes equidistant from the center.

4. Prepare your wick if it needs to be primed, and cut to the desired length. If your candle is very large, you may want to use multiple wicks, or prime a piece of extra-large wick.

5. Heat the wax to between 275°F and 300°F but no hotter. If you are using dye, do *not* add it to the wax at this point since these high temperatures tend to muddy the color. Once the first pour is done, and the hottest wax has been allowed to seep into the sand, you can reduce the temperature, add dye, and then repour the rest of the candle.

6. When the wax is up to temperature, hold a spoon or other implement to act as a deflector near the bottom of the hole and pour the wax over it. This will prevent the wax from eroding the shape you so carefully created in the sand. Pour slowly until the hole is full. The wax level will drop as wax seeps into the surrounding sand, making a shell.

7. Poke through the wax surface and refill the hole as necessary. When the surface wax has solidified to at least ⅛ inch thick, insert a wick through the wax, extending into the sand below about ¼ inch.

8. Allow 3–4 hours for your candle to cool, then dig under it and lift it out. Wipe off the excess sand.

Pour wax gently so it does not disturb your sand mold (step 6).

Sand Candle Variations

The possibilities for sand candles go on and on and on. Here are a few fun variations to try.

◆ Pour just barely melted wax into a compressed hole in the sand. Mix the wax and sand with your hands and press it to form the shell of the candle. When the shell has cooled, fill it with wax heated to 175–200°F, using a spoon to deflect the hot wax as you pour.

◆ To finish the outside, some people use a propane torch on the finished candle to fully melt the surface sand into the wax so the candle does not feel sandy and get sand all over everything. You can achieve similar results by holding the wick and overdipping the sandy surface in wax with a high melting point (145°F or higher) to seal it.

◆ Form several shapes in the sand, each with its own wick, and connect them with channels of wax to make one sand candle.

◆ Pour white wax into the compressed hole, then swirl a dark color on the surface as it cools.

BALLOON CANDLES

Yes, it sounds odd, but a balloon filled with water can withstand being submerged in hot wax! This method creates a hollow wax shell that is just the start of an interesting candle or an unusual candleholder.

Materials
◆ Paraffin wax
◆ Stearic acid to 10 percent of the paraffin
◆ Balloon (round is best)
◆ Water
◆ Color, as desired
◆ Scent, as desired

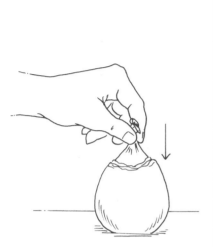

Flatten the bottom of your warm, wax-covered balloon (step 5).

Equipment

◆ Double boiler or concealed-element heater
◆ Bucket filled with water

1. Combine paraffin and stearic acid in double boiler or heater and heat to 150–180°F.

2. Fill the balloon with cool water and tie a knot.

3. Carefully dip the balloon in the paraffin, to cover one-half to three-quarters of the surface.

4. Allow waxed balloon to cool for at least 1 minute between dips into the wax, or dip in water between wax dips, making sure there are no water droplets left on the wax.

5. When the wax has reached a thickness of 1/8 to 1/4 inch, set the balloon down on a flat surface, carefully pushing and balancing it to form a flat bottom while the wax is still warm.

6. Hold the balloon candle over the sink and run it under cool water until it is completely cold. Pop the balloon and remove the balloon parts.

Finishing Options

◆ If your balloon-molded shell is thick enough, you can carve the top opening large enough to insert a votive and use it as a glow lamp. Be sure your wax lampshade is big enough so that the votive doesn't melt it.

◆ You can fill the balloon shell with wax and a wick. Put a primed or cored wick in the shell before you start pouring. The best way to make this candle is to pour in layers, or to pour in a little wax and swirl it around the inside of the shell like brandy in a snifter, building up a thickness slowly. You'll probably have to prop up the wick as you build layers in spite of its stiffness. Be careful about the wax's temperature. Your shell will melt if the wax is poured in too fast and too hot. I learned this the hard way!

◆ If you make the original shell without stearic acid, it will be more translucent than opaque. Then you can swirl colors on the inside walls of the shell, or pour multiple colors that will show through the shell.

A Hand(y) Alternative to Balloons

The dipping method that you use on a balloon also works using your hand. Use relatively cool wax (125°F). Dip your hand into the wax, wait for it to cool, then dip it in the wax again. Build up layers on your hand, then carefully remove the wax. You can fill this shape with a different color wax or swirl colors inside it to make an unusual hand candle.

Dip your hand only to its widest point.

MY BALLOON DISASTER STORY

Until I started research for this book, I had never heard of balloon candles, but the idea intrigued me so I thought I would give them a try. I set up my work area, filled my balloon with water, heated my wax to 160°F, and dipped until I had a white shell about ¼ inch thick. While the wax was still soft, I flattened the candle's bottom, then ran it under cool water and popped the balloon. Things were going great!

I decided to continue with the experiment and fill the center of the candle with red wax. I poured some of my white into a small can, dyed it red, and reheated it to 160°F. After placing a tabbed wick in the center of the white shell, I began to pour and watched my beautiful shell melt and collapse, sending liquid wax all over my counter. Luckily, I had covered my work surface with kraft paper, so I was able to peel the cooled wax off and remelt it.

The next time I made a balloon shell, I reduced the temperature of the wax for the inner color to 130°F and poured just a quarter inch at a time, allowing each layer to cool before pouring the next.

I still think of this experiment each time I consider making candles without taking the time to set up my workspace with paper coverings. Once I start playing with wax, I never know if I'm going to make a big mess, so it's safer to assume the worst and protect my kitchen counters.

MAKING MOLDS

Once you go beyond basic cylinder or block shapes for molded candles, you will need to use two-piece molds. Two-piece molds can be purchased or, with some practice, made at home. It is possible to make three-or-more-part molds for very complex shapes, but it is rather impractical for candlemaking since every seam increases the possibility of wax leakage and creates more seam lines in the wax.

Materials Used

Molds can be made of plaster, clay, natural rubber, latex, and silicone rubber. The model for a mold can be a sculpture of your own design or a found object, as long as it is made of a nonporous material. You might, for example, make a one-of-a-kind candle, with surface decorations, which you like enough to reproduce. Or you might be playing with modeling clay and create a shape that could be a handsome candle. Or you might be at a garage sale or a junk store and see a beautiful cut-glass vase. Perhaps a piece of carved wooden molding, a ball of string, or an apple strikes you as a starting point for a candle. Any of these can become the model for a mold.

You can make temporary molds out of clay, which you peel off when the wax is hard. You can wrap a form in plaster bandage material, leaving a hole to pour in the melted wax, then slice it along a parting line (the separation between the two halves of a mold). When the plaster is dry, rubber-band the two halves together, then pour wax into your mold. But if you want to get into reusable, high-quality molds, it gets a bit more complicated.

Purchased molds for straight-sided candles can be made of hard acrylic, natural rubber, silicone rubber, or metal. All of these materials work well as long as you use the appropriate mold-releasing agent and allow the candle to cool completely before removing it from the mold.

But what material should you choose if you want to make your own molds? Here are some general guidelines.

CAUTION

Each mold material comes with a specification sheet listing its attributes and instructions for safe use. Read it carefully. Nearly all of them caution users to wear rubber gloves and to be sure of proper ventilation when preparing the material.

Clay. Clay is used for one-of-a-kind art candles or to duplicate a shape you've created. Don't use clay for mass production.

Plaster. Makes great molds but it has no flexibility. You can pour candles with a two-part plaster mold and it will work fine, but in realistic production terms, plaster is used to make a master from which a flexible mold can be created.

Natural Rubber. A wonderful, flexible moldmaking material but it has one big drawback — it reacts badly to stearic acid. Over a period of time, stearic acid will mar the inner surface of a rubber mold so the surface of your candles will be textured and not smooth.

If you're going to make a mold that will be used only a few times, you can use rubber because the chemical reaction is a slow process. But many of the liquid plastics listed below look, feel, and act like rubber without reacting to stearic acid.

Polyvinyl Chlorides. Inexpensive moldmaking materials but they are not heat resistant. These are not ideal for making candles.

Latex. Used as a brush-on mold material. It is very elastic and a nice, thin-walled mold can be made by applying 10 to 20 coats of latex to a model. However, it shrinks as it dries and must be supported to prevent distortion. Latex is a good choice for great one-of-a-kind, odd-shaped molds if you don't mind if the candle comes out smaller than the original form and you don't expect to use the mold more than 10 to 20 times.

Silicone Rubber. An excellent mold material and comes in a variety of heat-resistant ranges. If I were going to use a mold over and over, I would choose silicone rubber for its durability and heat resistance.

Polysulfide. Relatively easy to use and can be poured over almost any surface as long as it has been coated with liquid soap or petroleum jelly as the releasing agent. Polysulfide makes a flexible, reasonably priced mold.

Polyurethane. Very inexpensive and easy to mix but it has a very short shelf life. Use it up soon after you buy it. In my experience, polyurethane molds do react somewhat with stearic acid over multiple uses but it can be used successfully as an inexpensive, short-production-run mold material. You should be able to make 10 to 12 candles before the texture of the surface of the mold changes.

Consider Draft and Undercut

The main concerns for a moldmaker are draft and undercut. Again, draft is the intentional taper given to shapes that aids in their removal from a mold. An undercut is any indentation or protrusion in a shape that will prevent its withdrawal from a one-piece mold.

If you can duplicate a shape you like in sand, draft and undercut become nonissues because of sand's flexibility as a mold material. Brush-on, flexible moldmaking materials also minimize the problems of draft and undercut since you can literally peel these molds off like a glove. However, you must realize that hardened wax is delicate, and you will probably not be able to peel a 1-inch rubber opening down over an 8-inch span of the outstretched wings of an eagle without breaking off the wings or tearing the opening!

If you choose to use a mold material other than peel-off rubber or sand, you will have to make a two-piece mold. The first step is to carefully determine the location of the parting line, the place where the mold will be separated into its two parts. Draft and undercuts must be taken into consideration in this process, since the parting line must allow the mold parts to pull away from the protruding areas or out of the indenting areas of your candle.

THE BASIC TECHNIQUE OF MOLDMAKING

Whether you choose plaster, clay, natural rubber, or silicone rubber as your moldmaking material, the basic technique is the same.

1. Look at the piece you wish to duplicate. Does it lend itself to a one-piece mold? In mold language, does it have draft and no undercuts?

2. If your model does have undercuts, you will need to make a two-piece mold. Figure out which direction the mold will have to be pulled off a finished candle in order to turn your undercuts into drafted shapes. If it is impossible to do this with a two-piece mold, I would recommend you choose a simpler shape for your first mold. There are several books on candle moldmaking that can help you with more complex shapes.

If the shape you choose to make your candle isn't somewhat close to cylindrical, your candle may not burn correctly. Many novelty candles are designed for whimsy, not for good burning properties. For example, I have a mold for a goddess candle. As my beautiful, buxom goddess candle burns, her shoulders and breasts fall off. The wick burns a 1-inch-diameter pool and her shapely parts sag and droop as her core melts. Bear this in mind when choosing shapes for molded candles.

3. Assuming you find a way to part a mold that eliminates undercuts, the next step is to find a cardboard box you can cut out the bottom of. This container will hold clay, your mold model, and your moldmaking material in place while you cast the two pieces of your mold. The box's width, height, and depth should be that of your mold model plus 2 inches or more. These extra inches will be filled with clay.

4. Place one of the open ends of the bottomless box on a flat, hard surface. Lay 1 or 2 inches of clay in the box to form a temporary bottom. Coat your model with mold release or vegetable oil to ensure it will not stick to the clay.

5. Place your model in the box with its flat base against one wall of the container so that no moldmaking material can come between it and the container. Since you generally pour candles upside down, the flat base of your model naturally forms the pouring hole of your mold.

6. Carefully embed the model in clay by filling the container with clay under and around the model up to the parting line you have chosen for your mold. Fill in all the space in the bottom of the container up to the model's parting line. The upper half of your model, the part above the parting line you've chosen for your mold, will be completely exposed.

7. Carefully smooth the clay's surface at the level on the model that matches the place where you want the mold's seam to be located. The more strategically this seam is placed, the less it will show in the finished piece. If it is possible to align the parting line with a texture or design line on the model, it will become almost invisible.

8. Embed several pegs or small beads in the clay around the model. These will become your mold registration slots.

9. Spray or coat the exposed surfaces of the model and clay with mold release. This should be petroleum jelly for plaster or silicone or mold release for rubber, latex, or silicone materials.

10. Pour your moldmaking material over the model and clay to a depth that will create a mold wall sturdy enough to hold wax without bending or buckling. Allow it to dry thoroughly. You have made one piece of your two-piece mold.

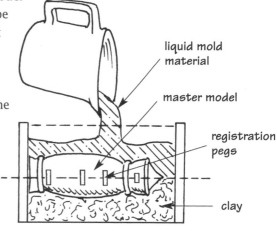

liquid mold material

master model

registration pegs

clay

Pour the top half of the mold (step 10).

11. Turn the box over and pull the clay out of the bottomless bottom of the container, taking care not to move the model and mold. Remove the pegs or beads.

12. Coat the exposed surfaces of the hardened mold material and the model with the appropriate mold release. Pour mold material into the container to a depth that will create a mold wall sturdy enough to hold wax without bending or buckling. You have now poured the second piece of your two-piece mold.

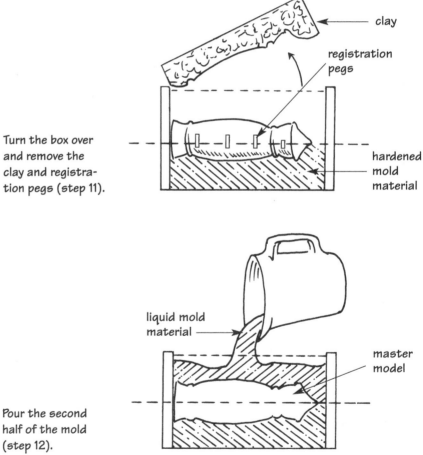

Turn the box over and remove the clay and registration pegs (step 11).

Pour the second half of the mold (step 12).

13. When the moldmaking material has completely dried, remove the bottomless box and your two-piece mold should split apart. Remove the model. The negative space it leaves behind is the vessel into which you will be pouring wax. The bottom of the model that you had pressed against the wall of the bottomless box is now the opening through which you will pour.

14. When you make candles with your handmade molds, you will have to hold the two pieces together with rubber bands or a clamp system.

Candle moldmaking is complex and exacting. It takes years of practice to become a master moldmaker. If moldmaking interests you, give it a try. Check the resources I've listed in the reading list on page 187 for more information. There is much more to learn than I have space to cover here.

CHAPTER 9
Dipped Candles

Dipping is one of the oldest methods of candlemaking and one of the most hands-on. It is the process of building up layers of wax on a wick. The dipping process naturally creates tapers. I remember as a child watching in fascination as the women of Colonial Williamsburg dipped candles methodically and described the skill as one of the many tasks of a homemaker in early America. Tallow, bayberry, and beeswax were the staples then. In addition to making the candles, women collected animal fats or berries and possibly raised bees to get the wax they needed. Today, most dipped candles are made of paraffin or beeswax or a blend of the two. Dipping harkens back to the early "rush dips," long, dried grasses that were dipped into grease and used like torches.

The basic dipping technique is simple. A wick is repeatedly immersed in melted wax until the candle reaches a desired diameter. Most of the time, candles are dipped in pairs. This means the wick is cut long enough for two candles, each end of the wick is weighted, and the growing tapers are kept apart by a spacer or frame. The frame keeps the two candles apart during the dipping process so they don't become attached while they're still warm, and the weights keep the wick straight until the candle's own weight does that automatically.

DIPPED CANDLES

The wax formulas and wick types specified in this recipe are meant to be guidelines. The relationship among a wax's melting point, the selected wick type and size, and a finished candle's diameter is critical in determining the successful burning characteristics of a finished candle. Remember to take notes so that you can repeat your successes or make adjustments for your next batch of candles.

Materials

You will need at least 6 pounds of wax to dip 3 pairs of 10- by ⅞-inch tapers, more if your dipping can is very widemouthed. Only about half this wax will become candle. The rest is there only to give you the depth you need in your dipping can to completely submerge the candles.

◆ Wick (medium-sized, 1/0 square braid, or 30-, 36-, or 42-ply flat braid)
◆ One of the following wax formulas:

Formula A
100 percent beeswax

Formula B
Paraffin with 5 to 30 percent
    stearic acid (I like 10 to 15 percent)

Formula C
6 parts paraffin, 3 parts stearic
    acid, 1 part beeswax

Formula D
Paraffin and beeswax mixed in
    any proportion

Formula E
60 percent paraffin, 35 percent
    stearic acid, 5 percent beeswax

◆ Color, as desired
◆ Scent, as desired

Equipment
◆ Double boiler or concealed-element heater
◆ Dipping can, at least 2 inches taller than desired length of finished candle
◆ 1 small piece of cardboard
◆ Small weights such as washers, nuts, and curtain weights
◆ Water bucket tall enough to submerge your entire candle
◆ Hook or peg to hang candles on

1. Measure a length of wick equal to twice the length of the desired candles plus 4 inches. For example, if you want 10-inch candles, make the wick (2 x 10) + 4 = 24 inches.

2. Tie one small weight on each end of the wick.

3. Cut a 2-inch square of cardboard. This will be your candle frame. Cut a ½-inch-deep slash on opposite sides of the cardboard. Fold the wick in half to find its center point. Align this center point with the center of the cardboard (1 inch in from edge). Push the two lengths of wick into the slashes. If you cut a 24-inch piece of wick, you will have two lengths of wick, each approximately 11 inches long, hanging from each side of the cardboard with a 1-inch space between them.

4. Heat the wax in double boiler or heater setup. The wax must be 10°F above its melting point — 155°F for medium-melting-point paraffin and stearic acid, 165°F if you used the beeswax formula. Add color and scent if desired.

5. Pour wax into dipping can 1 inch from top. Add wax as needed throughout process to keep at this height.

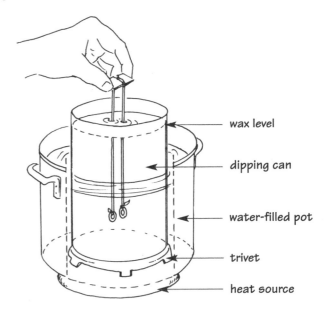

Dip weighted wick into hot wax until all the air bubbles exit.

6. Dip the wick down into the wax until just about 1 inch of wick shows below the cardboard. Hold for 30 seconds. This will allow all the air bubbles to leave the wick. Pull the wick up slowly and steadily when you see no more bubbles.

7. Hang the wick by the cardboard on a peg or suspended dowel until wax feels cool. Do not let the wick bend. You can speed up this cooling process by dipping the growing candle into water between each dip. If you decide to do this, be sure all the water droplets have come off the candles before you redip or you will have wax-covered water bubbles in your candles. These are unsightly and will cause the candles to sputter when you burn them.

8. When the wax feels cool, redip the wick. Dip in quickly, up to the same point on the wick as the first time, and pull out slowly and steadily. When the wax is cool, repeat this process once more. You should see a small wax buildup. If not, allow your dipping wax to cool by 5°F and do these two dips again.

It's a good idea to rotate your cardboard frame each time you dip to avoid bowing the candles. It also helps to be able to see the other side of the candles every other dip to be sure that you are getting a smooth layering effect.

9. Continue dipping all the way up to the tip of the growing candles, cooling between dips (the cooling time will increase as the candle thickens), until the taper is at least ¼ inch thick at its widest point. The candles will be heavy and stiff enough to weight themselves down at this point, so you can carefully slice off the bottom of each, taking the wick end and weight. The cleaner and straighter you cut the base, the nicer your finished candle base will be, but you can also repeat this process later in the dipping to form the finished base.

In order to reuse the weight, melt the wax off by dropping it into hot wax.

10. Continue dipping until the candle is the desired diameter, ⅞ inch being most common. Replenish the wax in the dipping can throughout this process as needed to maintain the depth necessary to completely

Cut off the weights when the candles are heavy enough.

ACCENTUATING THE TAPER

Dipping creates a natural, slim taper but you can make this shape more pronounced. Once you've dipped the wick once, follow these instructions for the next three dips.

1. Visually split the length of the candle into quarters. Dip the candle into the wax leaving only the top quarter exposed. Cool.
2. Immerse the candle for a second dip that reaches only to the halfway point of its length. Cool.
3. Make a third dip that covers only the bottom quarter of the candle. Cool. After the above dips are made, some candlemakers make a taper dip one-third up, and then two-thirds up, to smooth over the first lines. Try this if you find your taper lines are too noticeable.
4. Continue dipping the candle (full length) until it has reached the desired diameter.

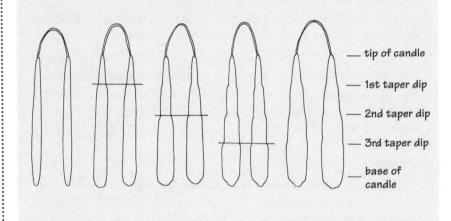

Make 3 sets of taper lines, ¾, ½, and ¼ of the way up the candle.

submerge your candle. If the base is elongated by drips or is uneven as you approach the finished size, trim it with a knife and proceed with the last few dips. These dips will round over the base, giving it a nice shape.

11. Some candlemakers raise the temperature of the wax to 180–200°F for the last two or three dips to improve layer adhesion. Some candlemakers use higher temperature wax, or a higher stearic acid content for the last several dips so that the candle has a harder outer coating and drips less when burned. In my experience, if you have the proper wax-to-stearic-acid ratio for the candle, this is not necessary.

12. If you want a shiny surface on your candles, dip them into cool water immediately after the last dip. Hang the candles on a hook or peg for at least an hour to cool further, then store flat and out of direct sunlight.

TROUBLESHOOTING DIPPING PROBLEMS

It takes time to become a master dipper, and understanding wax temperature is probably the most crucial factor in the process. Shaping the candles and avoiding surface blemishes are also difficult. Following are a few tips for diagnosing trouble.

While Dipping

- If your candle is not growing with each successive dip, if it appears to melt, or if the surface is blistering, the wax is too hot, or you are lingering too long in the hot wax.
- If the wax is thick and lumpy, the temperature is too cool.
- Because wax shrinks as it cools, successive dips should be of relatively close temperatures and the candle must be cool but not cold when you redip it.

Surface Blemishes

Surface blemishes can be caused by the wax being too hot or too cold. If the wax is too hot or has too high an oil content, you may get blisters filled with air. If the wax is too cold, it will go on lumpy and thick.

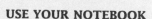

USE YOUR NOTEBOOK

When you adjust the temperature of the wax you're using to dip candles, note the adjustment in your notebook. That way, you'll know what temperature works best for that particular wax mixture. Each wax formula has different temperature requirements and I recommend taking notes if you plan to repeat different techniques. From holiday season to holiday season, you may not remember at what temperature you dipped those beeswax candles for your table centerpiece!

Dipping is perhaps the most temperamental of all candlemaking techniques. One aspect often overlooked is that of air circulation in the room while you are dipping. The center of the candle is hot and must cool before you dip again. Some people run air-circulating fans during the first two-thirds of the dipping process to speed up the cooling of the candle centers between dips; the cooling process takes longer with each successive dip because the candle is that much thicker.

However, deliberately creating a draft may cause surface blemishes, including mottling or tiny cracks, which are sometimes called cold lines. These are an indication that the top layer of wax and the internal core may not have optimal adhesion to one another. Cold lines may also be the result of allowing the core to cool too much and then shocking the candle when you submerge it into the hot wax. Or they may be caused by the draft in the room causing the outer layer to cool too quickly. These visual blemishes can be successfully covered by subsequent dips, if you control the wax and air temperature as you approach the last third of the dipping process. The air should be as still as possible as you embark on the last few dips into the wax. Turn off the fans and close the windows and doors!

Layer Adhesion

Good temperature control means good layer adhesion. Layer adhesion is the melding together of successive dips. Poor layer adhesion can result in a candle that breaks apart in concentric circles, like an onion. Good layer adhesion will produce a candle that's a solid rod of wax that will come apart only if intentionally broken.

If you are having problems with layer adhesion, try changing the following during the dipping process:

1. Lengthen the submersion time.
2. Shorten the time between dips.
3. Raise the wax's temperature.
4. Increase the ambient (room) temperature.

In fact, the four items listed above — submersion time, time between dips, wax temperature, and room temperature — are all critical. They should be recorded in your notebook and explored whenever you're having trouble dipping quality candles.

ARE ADDITIVES THE ANSWER?

There are a variety of additives on the market that may eliminate some of the problems encountered by candle dippers. Stearic acid, traditionally used to harden dipped candles to prevent them from bending, can be replaced with additives that offer the same characteristics but require smaller amounts of product. In addition, you can achieve a durable overdip by adding a hard microcrystalline to the regular candle wax, rather than using blocks of wax with a higher melting point. Other additives will eliminate mottling and bubbles on the wax's surface.

While some of the problems you encounter may be alleviated with the use of additives, the biggest challenge for the candle dipper is learning the correct techniques. The length of time the growing candles are allowed to linger in the hot wax, the cooling time between dips, the temperature of the wax, and the air circulation in the room are the most critical parts of the dipping process. Don't assume that additives will solve these problems; dipping candles by hand is more a matter of time and temperature than of chemicals.

What began as a simple, practical craft — rendering animal fat into fuel to produce light — has grown, through new petroleum technologies, into a highly complex process with numerous ingredients that give the candlemaker many choices. But these new ingredients force us to become amateur chemists in order to understand the impact of each additive on the finished product. Before you start dumping additives into your wax, take the time to learn the meditative art of candle dipping.

OVERDIPPING CANDLES

If you've ever watched a commercially made, dripless candle burn, you've probably noticed that the wax on the outside of the candle melts more slowly than the wax inside. This phenomenon is caused by more than the wax's proximity to the wick. Dripless candles are often overdipped with a layer of wax with a higher melting point than the rest of the candle. This lets the wax close to the wick be consumed by the flame before it can drip.

Overdipping creates a hard outer shell on your candle. Overdipping rolled candles in clear wax seals their layers together. This is not necessary but can give a nice, finished appearance to a candle, particularly if you have rolled a spiral design. You can also use a translucent overdip to adhere decorations to the candle's surface. For this technique, use paraffin without stearic acid. You can overdip  any candle you make using the same wax as the candle itself with the addition of 10 percent hardening microcrystalline. No additives are necessary for a beeswax overdip.

CAUTION

Before you melt the wax for overdipping, be sure to have headroom in the dipping container, since the candle will displace wax as you dip it.

Materials

- High-melting-point wax
- 5 to 30 percent stearic acid by weight (depending on technique; see introduction on previous page)
- Cool water (optional)

Equipment

- Double boiler or concealed-element heater
- Pliers
- Bucket

1. Melt the wax at least 20°F above its melting point.

2. In order to ensure good adhesion of an overdip wax, the candle to be dipped should be warm, not cold. Hold it in your hands until it is warm to the touch or keep it in a warm place until you are ready to dip it.

3. Holding the candle's wick with your hands or in a pair of pliers, submerge the whole candle in the overdip, then pull it out slowly and steadily. Work quickly so you don't melt the candle; be aware that it will be soft and pliable for several minutes. A second dip is not necessary but you may decide you want one to thicken the outer layer.

4. If your wax is not deep enough to submerge the whole candle, you can do half, flip it over, and do the other half. If your candle is a spiral with diagonal layers, overdip following the angle of the spiral to conceal the overlap of the overdipping.

5. If you want a glossy finish, plunge the candle into cool water immediately.

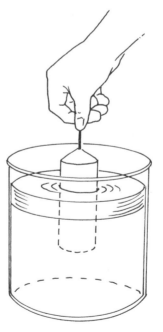

Pull out of the wax slowly when overdipping.

OVERDIPPING AN OUTER COLOR

It is not necessary to use colored wax throughout the dipping process. A dipped (or purchased) white candle can be colored by overdipping it in one or more colors. To do this, you must have containers deep enough to submerge the candles completely — one for each color. You have to melt a large quantity of wax for each color, enough to submerge the whole candle, in the above overdipping method.

There are two methods for achieving the overdip.

Method 1

1. Choose any wax formula from page 41. Melt wax either in your wax-melting pot or in individual cans for each color. Add color and scent to each can as you please. Many people use a small percentage of micro-crystalline hardener in their overdip formula, too.

2. Dip the whole candle, or part of it, in one color. If you want to have two or more colors on the outside of the candle, dip the large end first, then turn the candle over and dip the tip end into a different color. By blending colors at a central band of stripes, you can create some beautiful colors on your candles.

Method 2

This alternative can be used when you have only a small quantity of a particular wax and want to use it to color a candle by overdipping.

1. Assemble deep cans for dipping — one for each color — in a double boiler or heater setup. Fill each can three-quarters full of hot (at least 150°F) water.

2. In smaller cans, combine melted wax with color. Pour the colored wax into one of the deeper cans on top of the water. Keep the water hot so the wax stays melted.

3. Dip the candle through the wax into the water. As you draw it out, the wax will adhere to the candle. You have to work fast, because the hot water will start to melt your candle.

The drawback of this method is that sometimes water adheres to the candle and is coated with wax, forming a bump on the surface of the candle.

OTHER DIPPING PROJECTS

When you're dipping candles, you'll notice they're very pliable while warm. While they're in this pliable state, you can create some very interesting effects. I find the following twisted tapers particularly beautiful in beeswax.

Twisted Tapers

Dip candles as directed until they are about ½ inch at the base. Remove the cardboard and twist the two candles around each other. With your fingers, form the base into a ⅞-inch stem to fit in a holder, and you have a double-wicked twisted taper. You can overdip these twisted tapers to make them look more connected. You can make braided candles the same way, using three or more candles.

Twist the two candles together and form the base with your fingers.

Flattened Tapers

After dipping a taper to the desired diameter, flatten it with a rolling pin, leaving the base round so it will fit into a holder. If you grasp both ends of the still-warm candle, you can twist the flattened wax. Or you can shape these tapers into leaves or petals.

Flatten and twist a warm taper for this novel effect.

Wax Matches (Vestas)

If you are someone who lights a lot of candles at one time and has nearly burned your fingers trying to light them before the match burns down, you need wax matches, or vestas. A vesta is a wick coated with only two or three layers of wax that can be lit and used as a long match for lighting many candles. Vestas are easy to make. Follow the basic dipping directions, but make enough wax for only three dips, using medium-sized wick.

VESTA

Vesta was the Roman goddess of the hearth. She was worshiped in a temple with a sacred perpetual fire tended by "vestal virgins." These female attendants began to serve her somewhere between the ages of 6 and 10, for a period of 30 years.

Traditionally, if a girl could blow on a dying flame and respark it, she was deemed a virgin, since purity was symbolized by the ability to blow on the holy fire without extinguishing it.

Birthday Candles

These can be made in several ways. If you want, you can simply dip extra-small wick, 15 ply or smaller, the same way you do tapers. But because they are so short, you will find birthday candles are not efficiently dipped one pair at a time. Here are two other methods.

Method 1

Dip wick as if you were making a long taper (see pages 111–115). Once the candles have reached the desired diameter ($\frac{3}{16}$ inch is common), carefully snip the long candle into sections 3¼ inches long. Trim the wax off the top ¼ inch of each small candle to expose the wick.

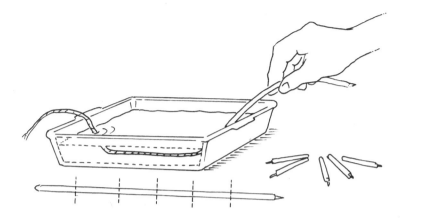

Method 2: Pull wick through wax and trim to size.

Method 2

Melt wax in a container with a wide mouth. Using a yard of wick, draw the wick through the hot wax, from one end to the other.

Repeat the drawing process until the wax is 3/16 inch thick. Allow the wax to cool a little between dips but be sure to redip while the wick is still pliable. Then snip the candles into 3¼-inch sections as shown above and trim off the top ¼ inch of wax to expose the wick.

This process, which is a variation of the drawn-candle method, can be particularly drippy, so be sure to cover the floor with paper before beginning.

DIPPING MANY CANDLES AT ONCE

There are many ways to do production dipping, limited mostly by the size and shape of your dipping can or tank. In addition to the cardboard-frame technique I explained in the basic dipping instructions, there are other frames a candlemaker can use to make space between candles so they don't stick to one another. Just remember, the more apparatus you use, the more wax-coated "stuff" you will need to snip and melt off.

A PERSONAL DIPPING STORY, OR
HOW I LEARNED TO MAKE SOAP

I grew up in the New York metropolitan area, and although I now live in a rural area of the Pacific Northwest, I am frequently reminded of my urban heritage. The papers out here often advertise farm-raised beef, so I decided to buy some. Not knowing what questions to ask, I answered an ad and agreed to buy one hind quarter of a Mr. Pedersen's cow, which was hanging in Butcher Boone's meat locker.

I arranged with the butcher to package the various cuts for my freezer and went to pick up my fresher-than-supermarket beef. When I arrived, Butcher Boone said to me, "Well, I've seen worse, but she was a barren heifer, and a fat one at that." He proceeded to bring out one box of meat and three boxes filled with huge chunks of white fat, for which I had paid the same price.

Determined to get my money's worth, I made 300 bars of soap. When I began to research this book, I remembered that I still had 10 pounds of fat in the freezer, so I set out to make tallow candles. I cooked the fat down on a propane stove outside the house, brought it inside, filtered out the crispy bits, and put it in my dipping can. At this point, my husband turned on the stove fan full blast because the tallow stank and the air was thick with grease.

I tried to dip candles with pure tallow. It didn't work very well though I'm sure it can be done. (I understand that earlier candlemakers processed their tallow with alkali and vinegar. I'll bet this helps.) Then I mixed 2 pounds of tallow with 6 ounces of stearic acid, 1 pound of beeswax and 2 tablespoons of a citrus scent recipe. Then I dipped two pairs of candles. They're soft and greasy, though getting a bit harder each day, burn beautifully, and don't smell too bad because of the added citrus scent.

Next time, if there ever is a next time, I'd do the complete project outside. I will also, in the future, ask about the lifestyle of the cow and talk to the butcher about the quality of the meat prior to buying locker beef. The butcher told me that next time I want to make soap or tallow candles to buy fat just for that purpose. It's a lot less per pound than the beef price I paid.

Live and learn. Country wisdom takes time to acquire.

Dipping-Frame Alternatives

◆ For one pair of candles, you can carefully dip a wick with no spacers or weights, pulling it straight for the first few dips, until its own weight holds its shape (A).

◆ Use hollow rods such as drinking straws and metal tubes as frames and make a continuous looped wick knotted inside the tube with spacers at the top and bottom of each planned candle (B).

◆ The simplest way to dip multiple wicks is to hang or knot several wicks over a rod that can be suspended between two poles while the candles cool. If you have a very large dipping tank, you will be able to dip an entire rod's worth of candles at once. If not, you can dip the pairs one at a time, moving the rod carefully in and out of the wax to coat each wick. Hang weights on each wick to pull it taut and halfway through the process, cut off the weights and melt the wax off them.

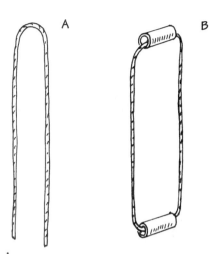

There are many ways to align wick.

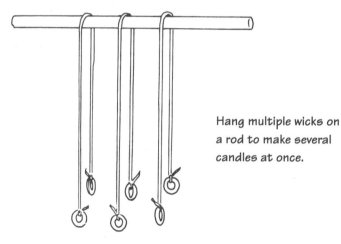

Hang multiple wicks on a rod to make several candles at once.

◆ You can buy round, metal dipping frames made to fit into some of the available round dipping cans. These have a central post with a hooked top like a coat hanger with four or more protruding rods at the top and bottom on which to thread the wicks. These are modeled after the romaine, a circular dipping system of old, used to

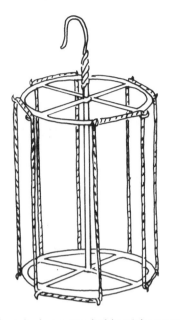

A wicked romaine holds wicks taut for dipping.

lower wicks into large cauldrons of hot wax. If you are handy with metal, you can make one of these from old coat hangers or similar-gauge wire.

◆ If you have an oblong dipping tank, you can make a dipping frame from wood or metal, with wick wound around it and spaced properly for the size of candles you plan to make. There is a set of plans in Klenke's *Candlemaking* (see reading list) that will show you how to make a frame that can be dismantled once the candles are large enough to weight themselves down. When the sides and bottom are removed from this frame, you will be dipping on a simple rod.

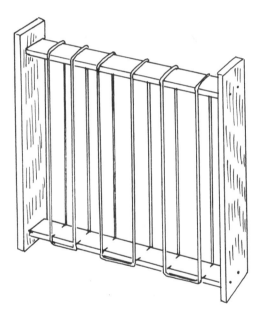

A dipping frame requires an oblong dipping tub because of its shape.

Any frame you use will become coated with wax that will have to be scraped or melted off. The more surfaces entering the wax, the faster the wax will be consumed, so be prepared to have more wax melted to complete the candles. Some candlemakers stop partway through the process and reclaim, by scraping, as much wax as they can to remelt for continued dipping. Depending on your frame system, this may or may not be possible.

If your candlemaking grows from a hobby to a small business, there are several dipping-tank suppliers who can help you determine your dipping-frame needs, based on tank size and shape. If you decide to get creative and weld your own tank or use stock tanks from a local feed and seed co-op, you'll probably have to continue that creativity into the design of your dipping system. But by that time, you'll be such an expert, you'll know exactly what you want and be able to find a carpenter or metalworker to help you!

Well, now we've covered the three basic candlemaking techniques — rolled, poured, and dipped. Now, on to troubleshooting your projects, then the fun of decorating your creations!

SUCCESS WITH FRAMES

It is wise to turn your frame around each time you dip it, to avoid bowing the candles. It also helps to be able to see the opposite side of the candles every other dip, to be sure you are getting a smooth layering effect.

CHAPTER 10
Troubleshooting

No matter how careful you are, you will occasionally make candles that don't come out quite right. This troubleshooting chart will help you identify the problem, its possible causes, and solutions.

PROBLEM	POSSIBLE CAUSES	SOLUTIONS
Dipped Candles		
Lumpy	Wax too cold	Increase wax temperature
	Candle too cold when redipped	Keep candles warmer between dips; redip sooner
	Wick not fully saturated during first (priming) dip	Hold wick in wax at least 30 seconds during first dip
Wax not building up	Wax too hot	Decrease wax temperature
Blisters, surface bubbles	Candle too hot	Wait until candle cools more before redipping
	Wax too hot	Lower wax temperature
Air between layers	Wax too cool	Increase wax temperature
	Candle too cool	Keep candles warmer; redip sooner
Base of candle getting tapered	Wax too hot	Lower wax temperature
	Time in wax too long	Decrease time in wax; add more taper lines at base

PROBLEM	POSSIBLE CAUSES	SOLUTIONS
Poured Candles		
Misshapen candle walls or hole in center	Shrinkage in cooling	Warm mold
	Not pierced and refilled enough times	Pierce and refill wick hole several times while candle cools
Won't release from mold	Wick still attached to the mold	Use more or different mold release
	Not enough mold release used	Use more or different mold release
	Repoured wax seeped between candle and mold wall	Repour carefully — do not allow wax to overflow in between candle and mold wall
	Poured too hot	Check, reduce wax temperature per mold instructions
	Stearic acid may be eating into the rubber mold	Don't use stearic acid with rubber molds
Air holes, bubbles (all causes listed at right lead to wax congealing before air bubbles can rise to surface)	Wax poured too cold	Increase wax temperature
	Candle cooled too fast	Use cool, not cold, water bath
	Wax poured too fast	Pour wax slowly
	Mold not tapped to release air	Tap mold before putting into water bath
Frost marks (surface of candle is mottled); cold lines (horizontal white lines around the candle)	Poured too cold	Increase wax temperature
	Mold too cold	Warm mold before pouring
	Too much stearic acid	Reduce stearic acid percentage

PROBLEM	POSSIBLE CAUSES	SOLUTIONS
Poured Candles (cont'd.)		
Mottled surface	Too much oil in wax	Use harder wax
	Too much mold release	Wipe off excess mold release
	Cooled too slowly	Use cooler water bath
Cracked Surface	Cooled too fast	Use warmer water bath
	Repoured wick hole too hot	Repour at same or lower temperature than original pour
Circle of bubbles around candle	Watermark	Be sure water bath rises to level of wax in mold
Layers not defined	Repoured too hot	Repour when previous layer is semi-congealed
Pit marks or dirt in surface	Dirty mold	Clean mold walls
	Dirty wax	Filter wax
	Poured too fast or cold	Pour more slowly and hotter
Layers not adhering or base chipping out	Repoured too cold	Repour when previous pour is semi-congealed but not cool
Burning Problems		
Flame drowns	Wick too small to absorb and burn off enough liquid wax	Increase wick size
	Wax too soft	Use wax with higher melting point or add more stearic acid

PROBLEM	POSSIBLE CAUSES	SOLUTIONS
Burning Problems (cont'd.)		
Drips	Burning in draft	Shelter candle from drafts
	Wax too soft	Use harder wax; overdip with harder wax
	Wick too small	Use larger wick
	Wick off center	Center wick carefully
Flame sputters	Water in wax or wick	Seal wick hole well to prevent water seepage
		Wipe bottom of pitcher before pouring to prevent water mixing with wax
		Make sure no water droplets remain on candle cooled by dipping in water
Smokes	Burning in draft	Shelter from drafts
	Wick too large; consumes wax faster than it can melt	Use smaller wick
	Air hole not filled well; trapped air in wax	Pour candle hotter and refill wick hole to eliminate air from inside candle
Won't stay lit	Wick too small to melt enough wax to fuel	Use larger wick
	Wax too hard for wick to melt	Use softer wax
	Wick not primed (saturated with wax)	Be sure wick is saturated with wax when pouring (no trapped air)

PROBLEM	POSSIBLE CAUSES	SOLUTIONS
Burning Problems (cont'd.)		
Small flame	Wax too hard	Use softer wax
	Wick too small	Use larger wick
	Wick clogged with pigment	Use oil-soluble dyes
Wick burns hole down candle center instead of burning out to full diameter	Wick too small	Use larger wick
	Wax too hard	Use softer wax
Flame too large	Wick too large	Use smaller wick
	Air trapped in wax causes wick to flare	Pour hotter and more slowly; tap mold before cooling to release air bubbles
Storage Problems		
Bending	Not stored flat	Warm candles and reroll flat on flat surface; store flat
	Not enough stearic acid or hardening micro-crystallines	Use higher percentage of stearic acid or hardeners
Chipping	Too much stearic acid	Reduce stearic acid percentage
	Candles not padded well; being banged around	Store in padded, safe place
Fading	Stored exposed to light	Store in dark place; overdip to recolor

PROBLEM	POSSIBLE CAUSES	SOLUTIONS
Storage Problems (cont'd.)		
Aging	Normal process	Polish with nylon stocking, with or without mineral spirits on it
		Remelt; filter and reuse wax
Discoloration	Dirty wax	Store wax out of dust
		Wipe clean of dirt and remelt, filtering wax

INDOOR AIR QUALITY

Over the past several decades, the issue of indoor air quality has been studied extensively, with regard to chemical emissions from permanent items, such as flooring and paint, as well as sooty deposits from discretionary items, including candles. Indoor air researchers are also finding candles on the market that release measurable levels of toxic chemicals, including lead (see Lead-Cored Wick section) and other compounds. With the increasing popularity of candles, there has been an influx of inexpensive, soft wax, highly scented candles that do not burn cleanly due to poor selection of wick, wax, containers, and additives. As a result, some people believe that "candles are the problem."

I believe that some candles may be a problem, but that is no reason to remove all candles from the market. Candles play an important role in our culture, and have for centuries. Candlemakers have to maintain a level of quality that will sustain the popularity of candles for years to come, gain the confidence of air quality researchers, and educate the candle-burning public.

As candlemakers, it is our responsibility to engineer our products to burn cleanly and evenly. It is important to be sure that scented and decorative products you use within the body of your candles have been designed specifically for combustion. When we develop new candles, we will undoubtedly make mistakes. If, upon test burning, your candles smoke and cause soot, go back to the drawing board and reformulate. Always test burn your products before offering them for sale.

What Is Soot?

Soot is a product of incomplete combustion of carbon-containing fuels. Research has revealed that some candles may produce up to 100 times the soot of a normal, well-formulated candle. These problematic candles may be the origin of some soot deposits in the home, resulting in a layer of black particles on surfaces, and the possibility of breathing problems from particulate in the indoor air. When a candle produces soot, it is an

POOR COMBUSTION

Poor combustion in candles may be caused by:

- ◆ Too large a wick, causing more wax to melt than can be combusted efficiently.
- ◆ Too much oil in the wax, caused by using too high a percentage of scent or a low quality, soft wax.
- ◆ Foreign particles or chemicals in the wax or on the candle surface, which were never intended to be combusted.
- ◆ Too little air circulating around the flame — often the case in poorly engineered, narrow-mouthed, deep-container candles — which prevents the flame from receiving enough oxygen to fully combust the fuel.
- ◆ Burning candles in a draft, which may prevent the flame from fully combusting the available fuel.

indication that the wick and wax are not properly balanced, or that there is too much scent or other additive, which changes the combustion properties of the wax.

Soot is also produced at higher levels when candles are burned in drafts or in an area where the flame is continuously disturbed by air movement. Soot is attracted to electrically charged surfaces, cool surfaces, and plastic surfaces, and tends to form deposits on ceilings, walls, and window treatments. Static electricity attracts it to electrical appliances, TVs, computers, and ventilation ducts.

Homes with a severe soot problem are said to have Black Soot Deposition, also known as ghosting, carbon tracking, carbon tracing, or dirty-house syndrome. Many newer homes are so tightly sealed that, unless a window is opened or a fan is turned on, the soot has nowhere to go but onto the ceilings and walls.

Producing Clean-Burning Candles

The cleanest burning candles are those made with hard wax, no scent, and a cotton wick. You can also produce clean-burning candles by following these tips:

◆ If you make a candle that smokes, extinguish it and throw it away or remelt it and reformulate your recipe.
◆ Trim the wicks of all of your candles to ½ inch to maintain a low, even flame.
◆ Avoid making candles with unusually soft wax or unusually high levels of scent.
◆ Don't produce candles in narrow-mouthed, deep containers.
◆ If a black ring of soot appears around the mouth of a container candle, it is producing soot that is not only depositing onto the container, but also rising into the air. Extinguish it and start again.

CHAPTER 11
Decorating

Now a new kind of fun begins! By combining techniques and mixing media, you can create candles unlike anyone else's or duplicate beautiful centerpieces you've seen at elegant catered affairs.

Warm the Wax

Before you begin decorating candles, be sure they are warm. They should be at least 85°F, warmer if possible. When I'm decorating my candles, I keep my waiting tapers and pillars near the woodstove or heater. In candle factories, they have a "warm room" set up with heaters and temperature controls to keep the wax at a constant 85 to 90°F.

TECHNIQUES FOR DECORATING WITH WAX

There are a variety of ways you can use special wax techniques for colors to put finishing touches on your candles. Here are a few specialized "wax-on-wax" techniques.

Overdipping

Wax for overdipping can be the same wax you use for candlemaking, with or without the addition of 10 percent wax-hardening microcrystallines. It can also be a wax with a higher melting point than the wax you used to make the candle itself. When used in an overdip, wax with additives or a higher melting point will create a hard shell around a candle. This not only protects the inner layer but also decreases the candle's chances of dripping because the outer layer will make a lip around the perimeter of a burning candle, keeping the melting wax close to the flame. Generally speaking, you should overdip a candle only two or three times.

If you are overdipping to cover flowers or other decorations, do not use stearic acid in the wax. This will make the overdip opaque and obscure your decorations.

You can overdip in beeswax, too. Beeswax has a higher melting point than most paraffins, so if you want a beeswax look on a paraffin core, submerge the candle two or three times in liquid beeswax. You can overdip beeswax candles with beeswax without any problems.

Overdipping also lends itself to several decorative techniques in candlemaking. You can color the outside of a white candle, create a series of colored stripes or ripples, refresh a faded candle, or attach decorations.

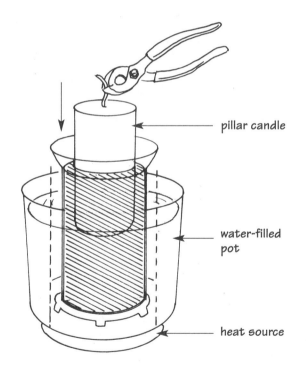

pillar candle

water-filled pot

heat source

Leave room for wax displacement when overdipping.

CAUTION: FLAMMABLE

Remember, when decorating your candles, flammable surface treatments can be dangerous! These materials must be used with caution. I've seen dried flower petals on a candle surface catch fire. This form of decoration is best used on a large pillar where the wax pool will be contained and the surface will remain relatively unmelted. I recommend these materials be used as decoration near the bottom of a candle, and the candle blown out before the flame reaches the decoration.

Please, never leave a burning candle — of any type — unattended.

OVERDIPPING A FINISHED CANDLE

1. Using one of the wax formulas found on page 41, heat wax in a double boiler or in a concealed-element heater. The wax should reach at least 20 degrees F above its melting point. If you use a formula with microcrystallines, note that their addition will raise the melting point of your overdip wax. Read the instructions that come with the microcrystallines to ascertain what that increase will be, and watch to be sure all the micro beads are completely melted. Be sure to have headroom in the dipping container since the candle will displace wax as you dip it.

2. The candle to be dipped should be warm, not cold. Hold it in your hands until it is warm to the touch or keep it in a warm place until you are ready to dip it.

3. Holding the candle's wick with your hands or in a pair of pliers, submerge the whole candle in the overdip, then pull it out slowly and steadily. A second dip is not necessary but you may decide you want one to thicken the outside layer or for depth of color.

4. If you want a glossy finish, plunge the candle into cool water immediately.

Creating Stripes

To make a simple stripe design with overdipping, wrap pieces of masking tape around the places on a candle where you do *not* want a stripe. For example, if you have a plain white pillar that you want to stripe with dark blue, apply the tape everywhere you want to maintain the candle's original white color. Now overdip it in colored wax, let it cool, and carefully remove the tape. To make stripes without masking tape, dip a white candle in one color (red) from its bottom to its halfway point. Turn the candle over and immerse it in a second color (yellow) from its top to a point where it overlaps the first color at least an inch. This overlap will produce a stripe of a third color, in this case orange.

WHIPPED WAX

Wax can be whipped to look like foam, or snow, or the head on a cold beer.

Material

◆ One of the following wax formulas:

Formula A
1 pound paraffin; 1 tablespoon cornstarch

Formula B
1 pound beeswax; 1 teaspoon turpentine

Equipment

◆ Double boiler or concealed-element heater
◆ Thermometer
◆ Eggbeater
◆ Spatula

Whipped wax creates a frothy effect.

1. Heat the paraffin or beeswax to 160°F. Add the cornstarch or turpentine and stir.

2. Using an eggbeater (which you will never be able to use for anything else), whip air into the wax. It will become frothy, like meringue.

3. Immediately apply it to your warmed candle with a spatula (which you will never be able to use for anything else).

A CHRISTMAS CENTERPIECE WITH WHIPPED WAX

Whipped wax can be applied to spherical candles with holly berries and leaves added as decorations.

1. Place the candle on a piece of foil-covered cardboard 8 inches in diameter.
2. Spread whipped wax all over the candle and foil.
3. Anchor the berries, leaves, or other holiday decorations in the whipped wax, out of reach of the flame. The whole candle will look like newly fallen snow.

Decorating with Sheet Wax

There are products on the market called Decorating Wax that are nothing more than smooth-surfaced sheets designed to be cut into shapes and stuck onto candles. Instead of pouring individual sheets yourself, you can buy a pack with 22 different colors to play with. Or you can make your own sheet wax for the following projects.

Millefiori. The millefiori, literally meaning "thousand flowers," technique has been used throughout history by glassmakers and is now very popular in the polymer clay field. These round, flowerlike motifs are created by making logs, or canes, out of glass, clay, or, in this case, wax. Modeling or sculpting wax, which can be purchased commercially or mixed according to the directions on page 42, works best. Or use a paraffin/beeswax mixture kept pliable with hot water or a blow-dryer.

The idea in the millefiori technique is to make long logs or canes of wax with a design running through their length. When the logs are sliced, each slice is a duplicate of the same design. These slices can be used as a repeat pattern on the surface of a candle.

With practice, you can make canes that look like faces, animals, feathers, and flowers. With some planning, you could sculpt a very detailed candle design.

USING MICROCRYSTALLINE SOFTENER

You may find that using a paraffin/beeswax blend does not offer the sculptability that your unbounded creativity requires. For increased pliability in sheet or sculpting wax, use a soft microcrystalline additive in the percentages recommended by your supplier. Refer to the Additives section on page 33 for more information.

MILLEFIORI STARTER PROJECT

Materials
◆ 1 pillar or other molded candle
◆ Wax: ½ pound (227 g) of paraffin; ½ pound (227 g) of beeswax
◆ Red and yellow color chips
◆ Vegetable oil

Equipment

- Double boiler or concealed-element heater
- 2 melting cans
- Thermometer
- Ladle
- 2 cookie sheets
- Cake pan filled with hot water
- Aluminum foil

1. Melt the paraffin and beeswax. Divide the wax in half in two cans and place these in hot water.

2. Add red chips to one can and yellow chips to the other. Stir well.

3. Prepare the cookie sheets with aluminum foil and oil (see directions for sheet wax on page 71). Pour one sheet of red wax and one of yellow.

4. Remove the wax from the cookie sheets when it is cool enough. Place one of the cookie sheets over hot water. Warm the yellow wax.

5. Cut a 1-inch strip of yellow and roll it on your counter to make a long, round rope.

6. Warm the red sheet. Place the yellow rope on the red sheet and wrap the red wax around the rope. When the yellow is completely covered by one layer of red, cut off the rest of the red sheet.

7. Warm the yellow sheet. Place the red and yellow log on the yellow sheet and wrap until there is a layer of yellow around the outside of the log.

8. Warm the red sheet and repeat step 7.

9. You now have a log or cane of wax that has a yellow center with red, yellow, and red concentric circles around it. Warm the log.

10. With a sharp knife, cut ⅛-inch slices of the log and push them onto the surface of the pillar candle, putting them next to each other as tightly as possible to create an overall pattern of red and yellow circles. This pattern can be continued all over the top and around the wick.

Millefiori surrounds a white pillar.

CHRISTMAS MILLEFIORI

Materials
◆ 1 pillar or other molded candle
◆ Wax: ½ pound of paraffin; ½ pound of beeswax
◆ Red and green color chips
◆ Vegetable oil

Equipment
◆ Double boiler or concealed-element heater
◆ 3 melting cans
◆ Thermometer
◆ Ladle
◆ 3 cookie sheets
◆ Cake pan filled with hot water
◆ Aluminum foil

1. Melt the wax. Divide it into thirds in three cans and place these in hot water.

2. Add red to one can, green to a second. Stir well. Leave one can white.

3. Prepare the cookie sheet with aluminum foil and oil following the instructions for sheet wax on page 71. Pour one sheet of red, one of green, and a third of white.

4. Remove the wax from the cookie sheets when cool. Place one of the cookie sheets over the hot water to use as a warming surface.

5. Trim each sheet so that it is 8 inches long. Cut two strips from each sheet, 1 by 8 inches. Layer them on top of each other, red-green-white-red-green-white.

6. Roll the layered pile on a flat surface to make it round.

7. Warm the green sheet and wrap it around the layered log, cutting it off after it encircles the log once. Repeat this process, wrapping the log in white and then in red.

8. You can decorate the entire pillar with ⅛-inch slices of the log or display the log slices as ornaments on the candle. To do this, cut very thin strips of green sheet wax. Starting at the wick, run them down the candle, ending them at different levels as if you were hanging ornaments at different heights. Cut slices of the warmed log. Shape these slices with your fingers into diamonds, ovals, rounds, and ogees. Push them onto the candle where they can hang from their green strings.

Use millefiori slices for decorated holiday candles.

FLOATING FLOWERS STARTER PROJECT

By cutting shapes out of pliable sheet wax, you can make flowers, leaves, and feathers that will float on water. If you sculpt the petals around a wick, you can make floating candles. You can use the flowers you make to decorate around pillar candles and make a centerpiece out of wax.

Materials
- Wax: ½ pound (227 g) of paraffin; ½ pound (227 g) of beeswax
- Wick (cored or 1/0 square braid)
- Green, pink, and yellow color chips
- Vegetable oil

Equipment
- Double boiler or concealed-element heater
- 3 melting cans
- Thermometer
- Ladle
- 3 cookie sheets or 8- by 8-inch cake pans
- Cake pan
- Aluminum foil

1. Melt the wax. Divide it among three cans. Color one green, one pink, and one yellow.

2. This project calls for thicker sheets of wax, approximately ¼ inch. Use 8- by 8-inch cake pans or bunch up the edges of the aluminum foil as barricades to make half a cookie sheet.

3. Pour a sheet of each color. These sheets will take longer to cool than the standard wax sheets, about 10 to 12 minutes. They can be warmed on cookie sheets placed over warm water.

4. Cut a 4-inch piece of wick. From the yellow sheet, cut five petal shapes measuring approximately 2 inches long and 1 inch wide. Squeeze the bottoms of the petals together around the wick, leaving ½ inch of wick hanging below the wax. Bend the wax to resemble the inner petals of a flower.

5. Cut five petal shapes from the pink sheet measuring 3 inches long. Place these around the yellow center with the pink petals squeezed together around the wick. Bend the pink wax to resemble the outer petals of a flower.

6. Cut four or five leaf shapes out of the green wax. Place these under the pink petals, extending beyond the petals to frame the flower. Use enough leaves to make a sturdy, solid, relatively flat base to keep the candle floating upright. The wick should be completely hidden by the green wax so that it does not absorb water when you float it.

7. Use up the rest of the wax sheets making more flowers.

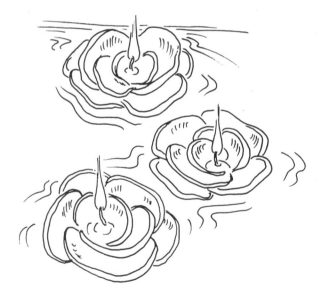

Handmade floating candles are made from sheet wax.

Flower, Herb, and Fiber Surface Decorating

Flower, Leaf, and Herb Appliqué. You can attach relatively flat bits of plants and natural fibers to candles with three variations of the overdipping technique. These can be pressed flowers and herbs or freshly dried materials. Do *not* use stearic acid in the wax since it will make the overdip opaque and obscure your decorations.

Begin by attaching the plant or fiber decorations by one of the following techniques.

♦ Pin the flowers, herbs, or leaves to the surface of the candle with straight pins.
♦ Dip the plant material in melted wax and then attach it to the candle while it is still hot.
♦ Heat the back of a spoon or use a heat pen to warm the surface of the candle and then adhere the plant parts or fibers to the softened wax.

Once the plant material is adhered to the candle, overdip the entire candle in clear wax. Be sure to pull it out of the overdip slowly, particularly as the decorations emerge, to prevent wax from dripping down the sides.

While the overdip wax is still hot, carefully push on all the tips and corners of the leaves and flowers so they are fully adhered to the candle's surface. Remove the pins. Overdip again to cover any prints and pinholes, then plunge the candle into cool water for a shiny surface.

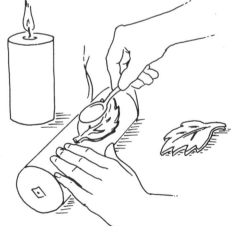

A heated spoon pressed against a waxed leaf adheres it to the candle.

Waxed Flowers

Real flowers can be dipped in wax and then applied to a candle surface. Traditionally, flowers such as lilies, fuchsias, sweet peas, orange blossoms, and roses are used for this technique. You can attach a wire to a flower stem or hold the stem with tweezers. Use paraffin without stearic acid since you want the wax translucent. Dip once, then reshape the flower. Redip by spooning melted wax over the leaves and stem. These dipped flowers are very fragile, so be especially gentle when you decorate with them.

Waxing Paper Shapes

Cut out individual rounded or pointed petal or leaf shapes from any type of paper to use as a form for waxing. Prepare and apply the paste or wax formulas (see page 42). Stick the waxed petals to one another with hot wax to form flowers.

   An alternative method for shaping leaves is to cut a 6-inch piece of wire and use it to attach several leaf shapes cut from foil. Dip the whole form in modeling wax. As you add layers of wax, use your fingers to squeeze and shape the leaf and petal shapes. Each successive dip will cover the cracks formed by bending the previous layer. A wire stem with leaves and a flower formed at the top can be bent around a candle or candleholder to create a lovely centerpiece.

A Little Bit of Lace

Openwork decorations such as lace, doilies, and paper cutouts that you attach to the surface of a candle, particularly a pillar candle, will allow light to shine through from the inside when the candle is lit. These decorations can be adhered to the candle's surface with hot wax, white glue, or spray adhesive.

CAUTION

Oil-based paints are flammable and should be used only on pillar candles because the wax pool rarely reaches the outer surface of the candle.

Apply wax to a paper shape.

You can also decorate a candle's surface with glitter stuck on with craft glue. Or try decorating with beans, beads, twine, or ribbons.

You can dip petal shapes cut from paper in wax once or several times. If you coat them with enough wax, you will eventually hide the paper. These shapes will become waterproof and can be used for candleholders and hanging or floating decorations.

Overpouring Core Candles

In candle language, a core candle is one that's smaller in diameter than the mold you intend to use. You can make interesting decorative candles by starting with a core when you mold your next candles. This technique works best with a core candle made of a low- or medium-melting-point wax and an overpour wax having a higher melting point or mixed with 10 percent microcrystalline.

1. Pin flowers or fibers to a core candle or set it in your mold and surround it with shells, metallic foil, or other decorative objects.

2. Using clear paraffin without stearic acid (you don't want the opacity of the stearic acid), pour wax into the mold.

3. If you pour slowly and steadily, you should not have to poke and repour. If the wax level does drop as it is cooling, simply add more wax to top it off.

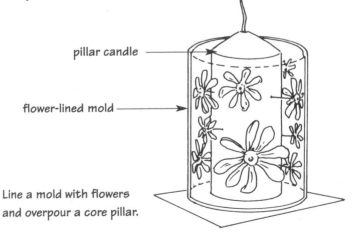

pillar candle

flower-lined mold

Line a mold with flowers and overpour a core pillar.

4. The closer the objects are to the surface of the mold, the more they will show through the overpoured, clear paraffin. If they do not show enough, you can melt some of the paraffin off with a propane torch, or dip the candle in very hot wax or very hot water, or carve with a knife or the curve of a spoon.

5. Once you have exposed as much of the objects as you like, buff the candle with a piece of nylon panty hose.

Embossed Sheet Wax

You can make a raised pattern on sheet wax with designs you find on embossed greeting cards, linoleum block cuttings, wooden moldings, textured glass panels, and shapes you make out of modeling clay or wax. Or you can make a silicone rubber mold of any nonporous, textured surface, like a floral relief on Aunt Blanche's tea tray, without destroying or having to purchase it. When you're done, you'll have sheets of wax with a raised design on one side and a flat surface on the other.

Once you start looking at the textures around you, you'll realize the possibilities for this technique are endless. It's a fun way to experiment with texture and wax to make one-of-a-kind candles, which may, in turn, become models for candle molds. It's a good way to make a prototype model without carving the design yourself.

1. To make a simple mold of a design, lubricate the pattern with mineral, vegetable or olive oil, or petroleum jelly.

2. Once the pattern is coated, squirt silicone caulk onto it. After the caulk is dry, carefully peel it off the pattern and you'll have a permanent mold that's flexible enough to peel off cooled wax.

3. Pour melted wax into these molds or press just-made, warm wax sheets into the molds.

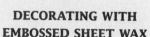

DECORATING WITH EMBOSSED SHEET WAX

This makes a great finish for a pillar candle. Measure the circumference of your pillar, cut the embossed sheet to size, and warm it on a cookie sheet over very hot or boiling water until it just about starts to melt. Wrap it tightly around your warmed pillar candle. The pattern you found on Aunt Blanche's tea tray is now decorating one of your handmade candles.

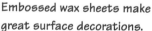

Embossed wax sheets make great surface decorations.

More Wax-on-Wax Techniques

You can embellish the surface of rolled candles with cutout scraps of the same wax. For example, I'm particularly fond of organic shapes and have created many candles with leaves and flowers made of scrap wax growing up their lengths. I've taught candlemaking to young people, who love to wrap candles in wax stripes of many colors. They sometimes make the candle very thick at the bottom by wrapping it in several layers that taper toward the top.

Decorating Candles with Paint. You can paint candles with regular colored candlemaking paraffin and stearic acid but it cools quickly and is difficult to manipulate. That's why most people paint with a paste wax paint made from wax and turpentine.

PAINTING WAX

Materials
- 1 part paraffin
- 3½ parts turpentine

1. Melt the paraffin and add the turpentine.
2. Allow the mixture to sit several days, stirring occasionally to evaporate the turpentine and leave the wax pasty. You can also heat the mixture to speed the evaporation process.
3. Add color as desired before painting a candle's surface using a paint brush (which you won't use for any medium other than wax!).
4. If you want a finish coat over the painted surface, overdip the candle in clear wax after you paint it.

Stenciling. You can decorate the surface of a candle by using a purchased stencil, doily, or piece of lace as a design template. Or if you'd rather, cut a stencil of your own design from paper heavy enough to wrap tightly around a candle and prevent paint from seeping through. If you want to stencil several candles, use waxed oaktag or acetate for your template.

Candles can be painted with acrylics, oils, gouache, stencil creme paints, and spray paints. Wrap the stencil around the candle and brush or rub paint through the openwork. Many people use a product called Rub 'n Buff, a metallic finish that gives the surface of a candle an antiqued look.

STENCILING STARTER PROJECT

Materials

- 1 white pillar candle
- 1 manila file folder
- Masking tape
- Stencil creme or acrylic paints

Equipment

- Sharp knife (an X-acto knife works here)
- Metal ruler
- Dauber made from a chopstick or dowel with a piece of foam rubber tied tightly on the end so the tip measures approximately ½ inch

1. Measure the height and circumference of the candle.
2. Cut a piece of manila file folder the same height as the candle and as wide as the circumference plus ½ inch. To make your stencil, draw or trace 2-inch stars on the paper at random, or use another a pattern of your choosing. Be sure to leave approximately ¼ inch between the stars.
3. Using the knife and ruler, carefully cut out the stars.
4. Wrap the stencil around the candle, overlapping the extra ½ inch. Secure the two edges with masking tape.

Make your own dauber to apply wax through stencils.

Make your own stencil from a manila file folder.

For more controlled designs, try stenciling on wax.

5. Work some stencil creme or acrylic paint into the dauber. Apply the paint to the open star areas, tapping the candle's surface with a straight up-and-down motion so paint will not creep under the stencil. Two or more colors can be blended directly on the wax surface with the dauber.

6. Carefully remove the stencil. Stencil creme paints need to cure for 48 hours before they are really dry. Acrylic paints dry in less time.

CHANGING THE TEXTURE OF A CANDLE'S SURFACE

You can decorate the surface of a store-bought or handmade candle by removing wax from its flat surface to create texture or by adding wax to the surface to build up texture. Either technique is also a good way to save a badly chipped or distorted candle. Or you can change a candle's surface by adding oil to the wax.

MOTTLED-SURFACE CANDLE

Adding oil to a candle's wax can be an effective way to create an interesting, randomly textured surface. The mottling result depends on the percentage and type of oil you use. Mottling is best done with a light, odorless or scented oil. Mineral oil (the kind sold in stores and pharmacies as a laxative) or vegetable oil works especially well in this decorating technique.

Change the surface texture of your candle.

1. Before you pour your candle, add the oil to the melted wax. To create translucent to snowy surface illusions, add 1 to 2 percent of the wax's volume in oil. To create crystalline shapes on the candle's surface, add 3 to 5 percent of the wax's volume in oil.

2. Once poured, do not cool the candle with water. The wax must cool slowly for the oil to do its job. The surface will look irregular but smooth-textured, and the candle surface, as well as the mold, will feel oily until you wipe them clean with a soft, absorbent cloth followed up with a buffing with panty hose.

Relief Designs with Heat. Using a heat pen or a piece of heated metal, such as a nail, spoon, or fork, you can melt away parts of the surface of a candle to form relief designs. The wax adjacent to the hot tool will become pliable and can be used to form raised shapes.

RELIEF-DESIGN STARTER PROJECT

Material
◆ 1 smooth-sided pillar candle

Equipment
◆ Lit candle, as a heat source
◆ Nail with ¼-inch head

1. Hold the nail over the flame of the candle until it is hot.
2. Starting at the top edge of the pillar, push the nail into the wax, pushing in and downward. You will be creating little round indentations with rounded, scalelike protrusions underneath.
3. Make as many of these as you can until the nail cools. Use this technique to texture the whole surface of a candle or create a spiral texture around the candle.

Carved Candles. Using fingernails, knives, a linoleum cutter, or another tool, you can carve away bits of a warm candle's surface and sculpt designs. If you have dipped a candle in several different colors to create layers of wax, your carving will reveal different colors, depending on the depth to which you carve.

Use a linoleum cutter or other carving tool to decorate the surface of a candle.

1. Work with a white candle warmed to 85°F or a just-dipped candle that's still warm and pliable. Overdip the candle in red wax.

2. Using a sharp knife, score diamond shapes into the red layer and remove the red wax. The result will be indented white diamonds on a red background.

3. If you dip the candle into yellow, then orange, then red, the surface will be red. But by altering the depth to which you score the wax, you can reveal white, yellow, or orange as you peel away the red outer layer. If you slice through the colored layers at an angle, you will reveal each color in a frame around the white diamonds. This carving technique works best if the candle is at room temperature. If the candle is too warm, it is difficult to get a sharp cutting line, and if it is too cold, the surface of the candle will chip.

CHAPTER 12
Candleholders and Related Items

A candleholder can be as simple as a bowl of sand or as ornate as a rococo chandelier. Regardless of what you choose, a holder must hold a candle steady and upright so that it can burn properly and safely. For safety reasons, I recommend that the part of the holder that actually holds the candle be made of glass, metal, or another nonflammable substance. This does not mean that you can't use wooden holders, but it's safer if you purchase metal inserts for the candle hole to prevent melted wax or the flame from contacting the wood. These inserts are available through many woodcraft catalogs.

TAPER CANDLEHOLDERS

In addition to the traditional holders and sconces for tapers, there are endless possibilities for beautiful ways to keep your handmade creations upright while they burn. Taper holders come in a multitude of shapes, materials, and sizes. You probably have lots of potential candleholders around the house. Once you begin looking, you'll be surprised by all the options (see ideas in box).

Be sure to use an appropriately sized candle for every holder you find. The most common candleholder has a ⅞-inch inside diameter. Even so, you'll often have to adjust your candle to fit a holder.

CREATIVE TAPER HOLDER IDEAS

- A knobby-skinned gourd with an appropriately sized hole cut in the top
- A flowerpot filled with sand or clay
- Fancy teacups
- Old glass bottles
- Widemouthed jars filled with colored sand or dried beans
- Old lamp with the shade and holder removed

Making the Taper Fit the Holder

Handmade candles often vary in size, and candleholders are by no means standardized. **If a candle is too small for the holder,** try one of the following methods for correcting the problem.

Drip wax into the holder to secure the candle.

◆ Melt some wax into the holder and hold the candle to it until the wax congeals.
◆ There is a product made specifically for this purpose, a very sticky wax that, when put on the bottom of a candle, will hold it in place by its very tackiness.
◆ Wrap the base of the candle with cloth or tape or (my favorite) the excess length of wick you just cut off a pair of dipped candles to separate them.

Wrap the base of a small candle to fit a holder.

If the candle is too large for the holder, it will look much better if you take the time to trim it rather than cram it into a holder and have to look at a chipped bottom the entire time you're burning it.

The preferred method for trimming a too-big taper is to score around the candle at a point up from the base that is equal to the depth of the holder. Then peel the dipped layers off the candle until it is narrow enough at the bottom to fit into the holder. The beauty of this method is that the candle maintains its full girth above the holder.

There are candlemakers who deliberately make candles larger than a holder's opening, and then trim the bases to 7⁄8 inch to achieve the beefy look and extra-long burn time of an oversized taper.

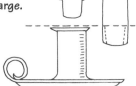

Score and remove layers from a candle that is too large.

To make a large molded candle fit, score it at a point up from the base that is equal to the depth of the holder and then whittle off the wax in small pieces (since it will not naturally break off in layers, as a dipped candle will). Try not to carve too much of an angle on the end of a candle or it will wobble in the holder.

CLEANING CANDLEHOLDERS

Some candleholders are meant to be dripped upon. Others are not. Some candles drip a lot, and some don't. If you're after the drippy-wine-bottle look, you can make soft candles that drip on purpose. If you're after neatness and sophistication, I recommend finding the right combination of waxes and stearic acid to produce a clean-burning candle. Also, avoid placing lit candles in drafty areas; even the best candles will drip in wind. Metal and glass holders can be carefully scraped clean of wax. Wax can also be boiled off the holder by immersing it in very hot or boiling water, and then removing the partially melted wax from the holder's surface.

Wax Shields

If you're really concerned about keeping your holders clean and simply don't want wax to touch them, you can use a bobeche, or wax shield. This is a concave disk with a hole in the middle designed to fit over a holder and catch wax before it reaches the candleholder. The candle is fitted through the bobeche's hole, then into the candleholder's hole. If any wax drips, it drips into the bobeche. Several companies carry wax shields, and they come in a multitude of colors and designs to match your holder. You can scrape or boil a bobeche to remove wax.

bobeche
(wax shield)

Protect your holders and
tablecloths with a bobeche.

DECORATING A BOBECHE

The addition of a bobeche, or wax shield, to a taper opens up a world of creative possibilities for adorning otherwise plain candleholders. You can start with a simple bobeche made of cardboard, coat it with wax, and attach flowers, bows, or other decorative items to it. You can make a bobeche out of plastic or sheet metal, as well. As long as you leave the few inner inches of the bobeche to act as a wax catcher, the shield becomes a blank canvas for decorating a candleholder. It might even be a reason to buy plain candleholders!

Just bear in mind that if you use flammable materials to make wax shields, you must exercise extreme caution when you burn candles in them.

decorative votive holders

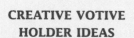

CREATIVE VOTIVE HOLDER IDEAS

- Widemouthed jam jars
- Clay flowerpots filled with sand
- Fancy teacups
- Cut-glass bowls filled with marbles
- Metal tart molds
- Fancy ramekins
- Wineglasses
- Translucent glass vases
- Small foil pie pans colored with stained-glass paint
- Inexpensive embossed drinking glasses arranged on a mirror

VOTIVE HOLDERS

The best place to find unusual holders for votive candles is your own home. The second best choice is garage sales. Just remember, holders should be made of nonflammable materials and small enough to keep the wax pooled around the wick so the candle can burn completely. In addition, votive cups are almost always made of glass to allow a candle's light to shine through.

Plain glass votive cups can be adorned by placing them inside decorative metal sleeves so the candle will cast interesting shadows. They can be placed inside translucent candle shades made of a variety of materials. The cup itself can be decorated with appliqué by fastening a photo, collage, or cutout stencil to the outside of the glass. A votive holder can also be decorated with stenciling or freehand designs painted directly on the glass.

Remember, as a votive candle burns, its flame is within 1 inch of the container's surface. Because some decorative materials will not be able to withstand this heat, run tests on the containers you choose for votive cups and the materials you use to decorate them. Be sure to use an appropriately sized candle for every holder.

WAX HURRICANE LAMP

When illuminated by a burning votive candle inside, a wax hurricane lamp resembles a glowing pillar candle.

Use high-melting-point wax so that the candle burning inside it will be less likely to melt the hurricane lamp and so that it will hold its shape over time. Do not use stearic acid, since you want as much translucence as possible.

Since a hurricane lamp is intended to be used as a candleholder, always use a votive cup or pillar holder inside it to prevent the candle from melting the lamp.

Materials
◆ Wax: 1 pound or less of paraffin with a high melting point
◆ Color, as desired

Equipment
◆ Double boiler or concealed-element heater
◆ Mold of choice, at least 3 inches in diameter

1. Plug the mold's wick hole, if it has one.

2. Melt the wax in double boiler or heater.

3. Fill the mold as if you were going to make a molded candle but do not poke and repour.

4. When the wax has congealed to a surface thickness of ¼ inch, break the surface and cut out the top carefully, leaving the ¼-inch side walls.

FT WAX

The hurricane lamp project is a good candidate for using FT Wax, an additive that offers a high degree of wax hardness while maintaining excellent illuminating properties. Since you won't be burning the hurricane lamp, you don't have to worry about finding a wick large enough for this high-melting-point wax. For more information on FT Wax, refer to the Additives section on page 33).

Pour wax into an unwicked mold (step 3).

Score the surface to remove the congealed layer (step 4).

5. Pour out the liquid wax from the center.

6. Allow the wax to cool fully before removing it from the mold. This wax shell does not need to have a bottom. If it has an open top and bottom, you can slip it over a votive cup instead of inserting the cup into the shell.

7. Decorate a hurricane lamp by overdipping or applying decorations to its surface, as desired (see chapter 11).

Pour out the liquid wax
(step 5).

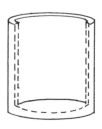

When cool, remove the hurricane
lamp from the mold (step 6).

Cleaning Votive Cups

Votives will usually burn until all that is left is a metal wick tab. At that point just remove the tab and insert another candle.

However, if your votive doesn't burn well and drowns the wick, rendering it unburnable, you will need to clean the cup. It's not a good idea to chip wax out of a votive candleholder with any type of tool since you're dealing with a thin piece of glass. Instead, set the votive cup in a shallow pan of hot water and slowly warm it on the stove over low heat. As the

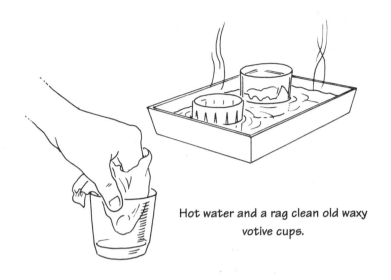

Hot water and a rag clean old waxy votive cups.

water heats up, wax will begin to liquefy and you can pour the glob of wax out and immediately wipe out the cup. If you want it spotlessly clean, submerge the empty cup in the hot water until the wax floats out of it, then wipe it clean. I do this to all of my votive cups periodically. It removes wax and the black charring that may accumulate from repeated lightings.

PILLAR HOLDERS

There are two principal types of pillar holders. One is a simple glass saucer with a raised lip around its edge to catch drips. The other is a spiked holder, originally called a candlestick because it was stuck into a candle. Neither of these holders is particularly exciting, but it's usually the pillar itself that's on display, not the holder. For variety, pillars can also be displayed on fancy plates, on an upside-down flowerpot, or in a bowl filled with shells.

Many pillar candles become candleholders themselves as they burn. It is difficult to make a large pillar that will burn cleanly down to the base. Many pillars burn down the center, leaving a shell of wax that glows

from the inside. When the pillar's wick drowns, the shell can be used as a votive holder.

CANDLEHOLDERS OF WAX

You can make very pretty petal-shaped holders out of sheet wax. These are perfect for displaying birthday candles. If you make these flowers at the same time you're dipping birthday candles, they can be attached permanently to the soft bottoms of the candles. Or you can keep the candles and holders separate. Of course, these wax holders are more fragile than the plastic kind, but I think they're unique.

A SNOWY HOLIDAY CENTERPIECE

Candles are particularly popular decorating items for the holidays during the month of December. Here's one idea for a candlelight centerpiece. You'll need:

◆ 1 tall, clear glass globe or shade (such as those used on oil lamps)
◆ 1 tall, cylindrical pillar candle in an appropriate holiday color
◆ Plate, shallow glass bowl, or foil pie tin to use as a base (must be larger in diameter than the glass shade)
◆ Kosher salt
◆ Holiday decorations such as ribbons, pinecones, and pine boughs

Place the glass shade in the center of the base. Fill the bottom of the glass with 4 inches of kosher salt and place the pillar candle inside the shade in the center of the salt. Arrange holiday decorations around the outside of the glass shade.

The coarse texture of the kosher salt resembles snow and, as the pillar burns low, prevents the candle's flame from reaching the base. If you use a foil pie tin as a base, it could be placed inside a basket without a handle. (A handle would arch over the lit candle.) Since the holiday decorations are arranged outside the glass shade, the danger of fire is minimized.

Begin by pouring a sheet of wax ⅛ inch thick. When the wax is still warm and pliable, cut out small petal shapes with a knife. You may do this freehand or trace around a stencil or pattern.

Join the petals to form flower-shaped holders, fashioning a point on the bottom of the holder that will pierce into the icing of the cake. Leave an opening in the top center of the flower that is large enough to hold one of your handmade (or store-bought) birthday candles.

CAUTION

Remember, if your holder is made of wax only, when it burns down there's nothing between the flame and your tablecloth, which is flammable.

Make your own petal-shaped birthday candleholders.

Other Ideas for Wax Holders

◆ Instead of flowers, shape the sheet wax holders into whatever object or form reflects the theme of your party — footballs, ballerinas, or bunches of grapes!

◆ Try using a copper plumbing fitting (a pipe end) into which a candle will sit as a base for a wax candleholder. Sculpt with any of the modeling or paste wax formulas to your heart's content, covering the copper.

◆ Dip live flowers and herbs into wax, then connect them to the base of a candle.

◆ You can make full-size holders out of wax too, as long as you're very careful to make them stable and willing to watch the candles closely while they're burning.

Copper plumbing fittings protect and hold a candle well.

LUMINARIA AND LANTERNS

Luminaria and lanterns are candleholders made of a translucent material that glows from the light of a candle inside.

The original luminaria were made of translucent paper bags filled with sand. A design can be cut in the sides of the paper bag, and a candle placed inside on top of 2 or 3 inches of sand. Placed outside in the dark, these can be quite striking lining a walkway at a barbecue or on the beach. But be careful! Those paper bags are flammable, and a slight gust of wind can set them ablaze. Use them outside only, have water nearby, and don't leave them unattended.

As every jack-o'-lantern lover knows, vegetables make wonderful luminaria. Any pumpkin, winter squash, or gourd will do, as long as it has a flat bottom and can be hollowed out. Even a melon or a pineapple can be carefully hollowed out for unusual luminaria.

The most striking pumpkin carvings I have seen are ones in which the outer skin is removed from some areas and the carver makes cuts of various depths. This allows different intensities of light to shine through. The effect is similar to candlelight deflected and diffused through an irregularly walled or cut-glass candle cup.

CHAPTER 13
Wrapping, Storage, and Repair

▼▼▼▼

Candles are delicate and easily damaged. The action of one candle rubbing against another candle can mar their surfaces. Candles stored improperly can bend, crack, melt, become discolored, or simply look the worse for wear. Taking some simple steps toward careful packaging and storage of your candles will ensure that they will be beautiful and useful to you when you need them.

THE PRACTICAL SIDE OF STORAGE

After your candles have completely cooled and have cured for at least 24 hours, wrap them up in soft, undyed tissue paper or similar soft cloth, foam, or paper. If you have a box that fits the candles snugly, put your creations in it as an extra precaution to prevent scratches and nicks to candle surfaces.

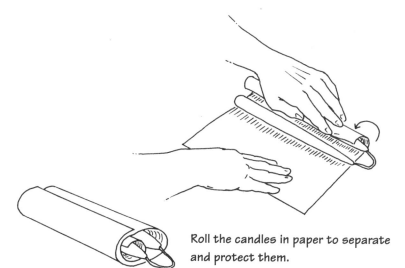

Roll the candles in paper to separate and protect them.

Storing Tips

◆ Candles must be stored flat. This is particularly true of long taper candles, which tend to bend if airspace is left beneath them.

◆ Store candles in a place that stays cool and dark year-round. Temperatures above 70°F for prolonged periods of time can soften the candles. If they are not lying flat, or not wrapped as individual units, candles run an increased risk of bending or melting together at these high temperatures. If wrapped and stored properly, candles should be able to withstand summertime temperatures.

◆ If you live in a very hot climate and have a cool or particularly well-ventilated spot in your home, this would be a good place to store your candles.

◆ Do not refrigerate or freeze candles. This can cause them to crack!

◆ Candle colors can fade if continuously exposed to light, so be sure to cover the box or close the drawer or cabinet where you store your candles.

◆ Candle scents can dissipate if the candles are not wrapped in an impermeable covering — plastic, for example. You have probably noticed that most scented candles come with a plastic or cellophane wrap. This is an intentional effort to ensure that the scent will be fresh and strong when you are ready to burn the candle.

◆ If you keep scented candles around, it's best to burn them regularly or to make them in widemouthed jars with lids so you can cover them between burnings to retain the scent. If left out in the open, scented candles will act as an air freshener, but will not emit odor when you finally get around to burning them. If this happens, add essential oil to the pool of melted wax as the candle is burning to rejuvenate the scent.

DECORATIVE CANDLE WRAPPING

Candles make a wonderful gift, whether you make them yourself or not. They are a great addition to gift baskets because they add color

**A LITTLE
HOUSECLEANING**

I have a few pillar candles in my bathroom so that when I have the time to take a long, luxurious, hot bath, I can do it by candlelight. If too much time elapses between uses, these candles get dusty and the steam from the hot water makes them feel sticky and dirty. So when I clean the bathroom, I clean the candles! I dust them, damp sponge them if necessary, or buff them with nylon stockings if they're scratched. They look so much better when they're clean, and I'm more likely to remember to burn them.

and texture and they're useful. I find that people want to be able to see and feel them, so I've tried to figure out ways to wrap candles that allow touching and still protect.

Tissue Paper

For a single candle, simply roll tissue paper securely around it and tape or tie with ribbon. To wrap pairs or multiple candles, roll the paper completely around the first candle, then insert the second one so that it does not touch the first, and continue rolling. This way, the candles are separated from each other by a layer of paper and serve as stiffeners for each other.

Cellophane Sheet or Bag

Since this wrapping material has the advantage of being transparent, cellophane increases the chances that a candle will be protected from scratches while its colors and decorations are displayed. Remember, the candle color can still fade from light that comes through cellophane.

True cellophane is made of cellulose and is, to its merit, biodegradable. However, this can work to a candle's detriment because cellulose will deteriorate if exposed to light. This wrap works fine for storage but has drawbacks if used for the long-term display of candles.

Fabric and Ribbon

For gift-giving, or for short-term display of candles, I like to wrap the bottom half of a candle in fabric or interesting paper tied with a bow. This allows the top half of the candle to be exposed so people can see, feel, and smell it. If necessary, add a piece of cardboard for extra stiffness before wrapping. This method works best for undecorated candles since the fabric wrap might cover or clash with the design of the candle.

Protect the candle bases but leave the tips exposed for a nice gift.

Boxes for Candles

If you choose to box your candles, be sure they fit snugly or that they are padded against abrasions caused by hitting the sides of the box. Some candle supply stores sell candle boxes for taper candles. The inside of the box has two holes for the bases of the candles.

If you're making candles and want a custom box, you can create one yourself out of corrugated cardboard or mat board from an art-supply

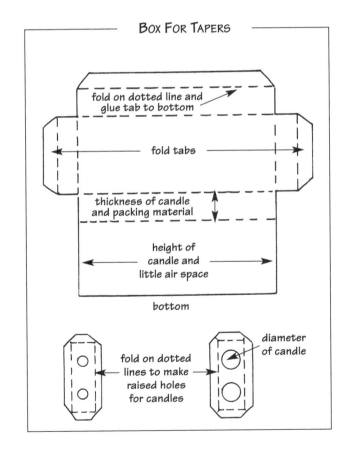

BOX FOR TAPERS

fold on dotted line and glue tab to bottom

fold tabs

thickness of candle and packing material

height of candle and little air space

bottom

fold on dotted lines to make raised holes for candles

diameter of candle

store. Here are a two diagrams for simple box styles. The first one is for a pair of tapers, the second is for a pillar. It's easy to make the insert for the candle base by making a raised bottom for the inside of the box.

If the outside of the box will be seen, use glue to fasten it together. Use masking tape if you're planning to cover the outside with wrapping paper or fabric.

Once you know how to make boxes, you can customize them for any craft project.

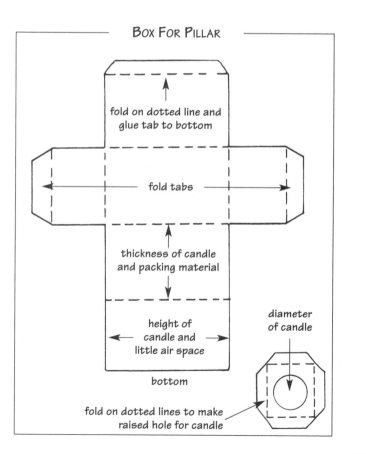

Box For Pillar

fold on dotted line and
glue tab to bottom

fold tabs

thickness of candle
and packing material

height of
candle and
little air space

diameter
of candle

bottom

fold on dotted lines to make
raised hole for candle

Gift Packages

Theme gifts are a fun way to give your candles away. These can be based on colors, scents, holidays, or other celebrations. A gift basket for someone who loves purple might include purple hand-dipped tapers, a lavender-scented pillar, some fresh or dried lavender flowers tied with a fabric bow, and perhaps a candleholder.

Holidays. Before the holidays, make candle sets appropriate for Hanukkah, Advent, Christmas, or Kwanzaa in appropriate colors and quantities to light for each night of these ongoing holidays. They make great gifts, if given early enough for people to plan their rituals with family and friends.

Treat yourself to a new candle mold from your favorite candle supplier and during a marathon candlemaking session, make a candle for everyone on your gift list for the entire year. You won't have to think about gifts for a while, and you can customize the colors and scents to individual tastes.

New Baby. You can make a perpetual birthday candle for new parents. Start with a tall pillar candle in white. Decorate the surface with a line and some decorations with paint or sheet wax appliqués for each of the 18 birthdays their new baby will have as he or she grows. The candle can be burned for about an hour each year for 18 years. Include in the new baby gift box or basket some elegant tapers with a note reminding the couple to take the time to respark the light of romance in their lives with a candlelit dinner for just the two of them.

Halloween. A child's Halloween gift might be a pumpkin to carve, some purchased tea lights or votives for inside the pumpkin, orange and black dipped tapers for a holiday dinner table, and a ghost candle made by sculpting warm white wax around a wick, then adding black dots for eyes. Include the safety tips on page 181.

BASIC CANDLE REPAIR

Should your candles become unsightly or unusable, try one of the following techniques for making them usable again.

Straightening

If your candles are bent, warm them in your hands, near a heater, or with a hair dryer, and roll them on a flat surface to straighten them. This method can also be used to flatten lumps on a candle's surface.

Overdipping

If the color is faded, overdip the candles in 180°F wax. Clean the candle first so that you are not permanently embedding dust under the over-layer. If the candle is very discolored, try dipping it into a dark color, or into a series of stripes, to mask the discoloration.

Buffing

If the surface is scratched or no longer shiny, buff the candle with a taut piece of nylon stocking. If necessary, you can use some mineral spirits, which will slightly soften the wax and fill in the deeper scratches.

Decorate the Surface

If a candle is dented or chipped badly, you can redecorate it, hiding problems under a new surface. If all hope is lost and the candle is beyond repair, remelt it and make new candles!

CHAPTER 14:
Moving into Production

I believe that candlemaking is as much a mental art as it is a mechanical one. It requires focus, deliberate timing, and attention to detail. As you master the finer points of making candles, you may want to step up the pace and produce larger quantities. If you do, new issues will present themselves. How much wax can you melt at one time? Should you buy wholesale quantities at lower prices? Should you buy wax by the box, the pallet, or the truckload? What kind of packaging will keep your candles safe during shipping and handling?

Besides the questions of quantity, there will be questions of quality and questions of sanity. Are your production methods consistently reproducible? Do you have the temperament to make the same thing over and over again? Do you want each and every candle to be hand-made? Can you automate some phases of production? As you can see, there are many things to consider.

VOLUME PRODUCTION

It's perfectly normal for new problems to arise as you try to speed up the production process by making multiple candles at once. It's one thing to carefully control the bubbles on one or two candles, but as you try to pour or dip 300 candles a day, you may be confronted with consistent problems that must be solved by truly understanding their causes. You simply won't have time to pamper each candle. You'll have to know that your production methods work and, if they don't, you'll have to find the reasons why in order to work toward a solution. And you'll have to be able to train employees to produce the same caliber of candles that you have lovingly developed.

Temperature Problems

In order to produce candles successfully, you need to be aware of the temperature in the room as well as any drafts wafting through. You may need to control the temperature in an area of a room in order to heat candles before you overdip them or to heat containers before you pour wax into them. You may even need to control the exact temperature of an entire room if the climate swing in your locale is severe or has extremely high humidity.

Perhaps you once heated containers with your hair dryer but now you need five dozen glasses heated to the same temperature at the same time. In that case, you may want to consider building a fire-safe box with interior shelving and a small heater connected to a thermostat at one end. It may need a fan to circulate the heat, so the glasses at one end don't get hotter than the ones at the other end.

Making Many Candles at Once

Maybe you used to dip candles in a double boiler on the stove and hang them from the coffee mug rack over the kitchen counter. You were able to melt 6 pounds of wax in one vessel, keep another 4 pounds on the back burner to refill the dipping pot as needed, and make a dozen pairs of candles at one time. But now you want to make 12 dozen pairs at once, so you need a way to melt 120 pounds of wax. It won't fit in your kitchen. Are you really going to dip them one pair at a time? You may need to design or purchase a rack system that allows you to dip multiple candles at once.

If you want to make molded candles in production, you must first recognize that the number of molds you own and the time it takes for each candle to cool inside the mold is directly proportionate to how many candles you can produce in one day. You'll need to make decisions about how many molds to purchase based on available funds, table space, and wax-melting capacity. You may be wicking enough molds to warrant buying a separate spool of wick for each mold; then you can strategically place it on a shelf above each mold with a screw-eye on the edge of the shelf to hold it in place.

To speed up the cooling process, perhaps you'll design a water bath in a vessel large enough to hold multiple molds. But how will you keep the water cool as you add more and more hot candles to it? If you are producing enough candles of one color to keep that color wax hot all day long, it will be available for repouring into candles that have cavities requiring additional wax as they cool. But if your production schedule is smaller, maybe you will you need two vats, one to keep the morning's color hot for repours and the other for a second color to be used for the afternoon's production.

Okay, so you can work through all of the production details, right? But now, if there is a problem, it's a problem in 12 dozen candles, not just in 12. I can't predict what your dilemma may be, but I can tell you a little story. . .

FROM KITCHEN TO COMMERCE

Several years ago in late summer I received a phone call from two men in Boston who had opened a small candle manufacturing company after successfully creating a line of taper candles on their kitchen stove. They said they were desperate: They had produced samples, gone to a major gift show, and taken orders for the upcoming holiday season.

Starting a Business

In shifting from small to large scale, they had rented a loft space and purchased several large wax-melting vats and many romaine-type dipping racks. Their formula was straightforward — a mixture of beeswax, paraffin, color chips, and scent. Gary, in charge of operations and staffing, had found suppliers for raw materials, hired employees, and set up the company's scheduling and daily operations. But Brian, who actually dipped the candles, was having problems making the shift from stove-top to production. Visual blemishes on the candles were rendering 50 percent of their daily production second quality. Brian was questioning his confidence as a candle dipper, and Gary feared that they might miss their first delivery date, disappointing new customers and putting their new venture at grave economic risk.

They sent me some examples of the problem. The candles were beautifully colored, subtly scented, and wrapped in some of the most beautiful candle packaging I had ever seen. The candles burned well, so I knew that the wick-to-wax balance was fine. But the bumps and blemishes had to go, and it was my job to figure out what was causing them. I had my suspicions about the sources of their problems, but we agreed that I should watch them dipping candles to get the real picture of exactly what was going wrong and why. So off I went to Boston unsure of whether I could help them.

Observing the Problem

On my first day I watched Brian dip. I monitored the temperature gauge of the melting vats and periodically inserted a thermometer into them, measuring the temperature at both the top and the bottom of the liquid. I asked many questions about the raw materials, their formula, and their suppliers. Gary and I watched each time Brian lifted a romaine out of the wax and pinpointed exactly when the cold lines and bumps appeared. At the end of the day, I asked Brian to prepare the wax batches for the next day to make sure that the wax would be at the proper temperature in the morning. I told him that I was going to monitor each dip into the wax and help him make adjustments throughout the next day's production. It was my hope that if we were successful, over 90 percent of tomorrow's candles would be first quality.

As I slipped off to sleep that night, I didn't think the problems were insurmountable. Nor did I think Brian would need additives or special equipment. He had already done an admirable job of formulation, but he had to change his mindset from the kitchen to the manufacturing facility. I was almost certain that his dilemma was partly a matter of temperature and air circulation and partly a matter of technique and mental focus.

Temperature

When we arrived the next morning, we discovered that there was a difference between the vat's thermometer and the hand-held thermometer that we dipped halfway into the vat, because the vat thermometer was located at the bottom of the tank. We would have to spend the day checking these two temperatures against each other, which would help Brian determine what temperature the vat thermometer should read in order to give him the desired wax temperature for dipping at the top and the middle of the tank.

As I watched Brian dip, I realized that he allowed the candles to linger in the wax longer than I thought wise. He also told me that he often had to dip 40 to 50 times to produce a ⅞-inch-diameter taper. If the dipping wax is at the proper temperature, a ⅞-inch taper should take 25 to 35 dips to build. We worked on temperature control, checking the wax frequently to be sure it was within 5°F of the desired dipping temperature. Brian had to learn the nuances of his new dipping vat and how to maintain the desired temperature.

We worked on the temperature of the candles, too. If they are too hot when you dip them, they will not accept a new layer of wax — they'll emerge from the hot wax the same size as they were when submerged. Most people dip them too hot and end up dipping many more times than necessary.

Production

A production dipper must also determine the number of racks that can be dipped in the same session. One rack should be cooling while a second one is being dipped. After all of the racks have been dipped, the first rack should then be cool enough, but not too cool, for its next dip. If the candles are too cold, the new layer will crackle with visible cold lines. That's why it's important not to leave for an hour-long lunch; the candles will get too cold to be redipped, and the only remedy for that is to place them in a warm room to increase their internal temperature so that they won't be shocked upon redipping.

Timing

In addition to temperature and production dipping, we worked on timing. There is a rhythm to each dip that comes naturally after you have dipped enough candles. The candles must be in the wax for as little time as possible, because too much heat can cause the inner layers to bubble, resulting in surface bumps. I showed Brian how to move with a very smooth in-and-out motion that does not ripple the surface of the hot wax, which causes drips. Brian practiced carefully plunging the racks into the wax quickly and pulling them out smoothly, taking a deep breath before dipping. He also noticed that if he pulled out of the hot wax too quickly, the tips of the candles became narrow, lacking enough time to allow a new layer to adhere. But if he allowed the candles to remain in the wax for too long, the bottoms became narrow because the new layer began to melt off. As a result of these insights, many of the bumps and drips he had experienced previously did not occur.

However, if Brian lost his concentration, he could see the results on each candle. I kept repeating the mantra, "Focus. Become one with the wax." And when he did focus, the candles emerged from the wax looking smooth, somewhere between 1/32 and 1/16 of an inch thicker with each dip, and still first quality. A master candle dipper learns to "read" the wax and the candles, and can adjust time and temperature to prevent problems.

Air Circulation

Finally, we worked on air circulation. As the candles got larger, some surface lines appeared. I looked around the room and realized that the window and door were open, causing a minor cross draft. We closed the window and the door and the lines disappeared. Then we were able to turn up the wax temperature for the last few dips to cover and seal the cold lines that had occurred before we discovered and remedied the air circulation problem.

Finding Solutions

By the time we finished dipping the 28 racks of candles, we had many first-quality candles and Brian understood what had gone wrong on the two or three racks that contained seconds. Temperature, timing, or technique had caused all of the problems. Some had been dipped too hot or for too long, while others had drips caused by early rippling of the wax surface. The drips had become amplified, enlarged by each successive dip into the wax.

Brian's production problems were solved without expense by using common sense, mental focus, and simple mechanical adjustments. It wasn't necessary to reformulate recipes or purchase different equipment; he just had to adjust his methods for producing in volume. Later that day he said, "This is amazing. Dipping really is an art, not a mechanical act. I was getting frustrated with the repetitiveness of it, feeling like a machine, but now I understand that each dip matters, and how important the human aspect of candle dipping is in creating beautiful candles."

A Happy Ending

Now, several years later, Aunt Sadie's Candlestix is a thriving manufacturer in Boston's south end, with Gary, Brian, and 10 employees producing more than 250,000 pairs of candles annually, which are sold in over 1,400 stores as well as their own retail store. Gary expertly handles the business operations, inventory, marketing, shipping, and staffing, and Brian manages production and trains dippers in the art of making finely crafted taper candles. It was a pleasure for me to be able to help them make the transition from their kitchen to a successful production company with a fine product.

PRODUCT DEVELOPMENT

As Brian now knows, product development doesn't end when you make the perfect prototype. Rather, product development continues until you have translated your prototype design into sound production methods. This involves making decisions about materials, equipment, and technique, as well as working through the new issues that develop as you begin to produce candles in greater quantities. I caution you against preselling any candles you make from a prototype: You need to be sure that you can produce them in volume before you make promises to customers.

Don't be discouraged; many kitchen candlemakers have successfully moved from hobby to production. As with each phase of learning candlemaking, the move into production requires careful planning and a willingness to work through problems. But unlike hobby candlemaking, your reputation is on the line, so it is essential that you are able to deliver what you promise. Doing a careful job of product development, from prototype to production, is the key.

LABELING YOUR CANDLES

Because of indoor air quality concerns, many candle companies label their candles with burning instructions, which vary among candle types. Some suppliers of raw materials have also begun to offer preprinted labels to candlemakers, so that small-scale candle crafters can label their wares for safety, while covering themselves against liability lawsuits. In general, all of these labels warn the user of the following:

◆ To never leave a burning candle unattended
◆ To never burn candles in a draft
◆ To always keep burning candles out of reach of children and pets
◆ To always keep candle wicks trimmed to ¼ inch to prevent smoking and soot build-up

Votive candles may be labeled with a reminder that they will burn for the stated length of time if they are burned inside a votive cup, which retains the liquid wax within the burning radius of the wick. Pillars may contain a warning to blow them out after 3 to 4 hours and to build up the outer walls of the pillars before relighting them. Candles that resemble food, such as a beer stein or fruit, may be labeled as being inedible. Gel candles often carry a warning to extinguish and discard them when there is ½ inch of gel remaining in the container.

With the litigious tendencies of today's society, even candlemakers are arming themselves against lawsuits. While it may seem obvious that burning candles have the potential to cause fires, we can protect ourselves and our customers by reminding them of the potential dangers of open flames in the home and how to keep hazards to a minimum.

CONCLUSION

I've come full circle in my discussion of the practical art of candlemaking as I conclude this chapter. Now that we've come to the end of this book, I think you'll agree wax is an amazing material. It's a fuel and a sculpting medium. It's completely recyclable, waterproof, and relatively inexpensive.

Candles are valued for their beauty, their light, and their symbolic importance for all humanity. For me, and I hope for you, there is tremendous satisfaction in creating useful objects like candles that are pleasing to the senses and a joy to share with others.

One last note: I would like to stress that each type of candlemaking is an art unto itself, and few people are experts in all phases of the art. Explore the techniques. Ask lots of questions. Ask the same questions of many people. I guarantee that you will get a variety of answers, and that one or a combination of them will work for you. Each variable in the candlemaking craft — the wax, the wick, the size, the type of candle — will have an effect on the burning characteristics of the finished candle. If you want to become expert at a particular facet of candlemaking, keep a notebook of formulas, temperatures, techniques, and change one thing at a time to check and recheck the quality. In the long run, your final product will be better if you take the time to experiment and find the best solution to your creative endeavors.

"Hope, like the gleaming taper's light,
Adorns and cheers our way;
And still, as darker grows the night,
Emits a brighter ray."

— Oliver Goldsmith,
The Captivity, An Oratorio

SUPPLIERS

The Internet offers hundreds of sites for candlemakers, including suppliers, project instructions, candlemaking kits, chat rooms, and links to related fields. Enter the word "candlemaking" into any search engine and you'll be virtually connected to the world wide candlemaking web. This is by no means a complete list. Consult your local *Yellow Pages* or the *Thomas Register* (at your local library or www.thomasregister.com) under "wax" or "petroleum products." You can purchase smaller quantities (under 50 pounds) from craft or candle suppliers. Most wax suppliers have a one-case (55-pound) minimum.

General Candlemaking Supplies

Aztec International
800-369-5357
www.buywax.com

Betterbee
800-632-3379
www.betterbee.com
Beeswax candlemaking supplies

Bitter Creek Candle Supply
877-635-8929
www.candlesupply.com

Candle Cocoon
608-233-9290
www.candlecocoon.com

Candlechem Company
508-586-1880
www.candlechem.com

The Candlemaker
888-251-4618
www.thecandlemaker.com

Candle Maker's Supplies
+44-0-20-7602-40312
www.candlemakers.co.uk

Alberta Beeswax & Candle Supplies
888-979-0909
www.candlesandbeeswax.com

The Candlewic Company
800-368-3352
www.candlewic.com
Complete line of candlemaking supplies

Dadant and Sons, Inc.
888-922-1293
www.dadant.com
Beeswax

Dick Blick
800-828-4548
www.dickblick.com
Complete art supply catalog, beeswax rolling sheets, and mold-making materials

Earth Guild
800-327-8448
www.earthguild.com
All you'll need to get started

From Nature with Love
800-520-2060
www.fromnaturewithlove.com

Georgie's Ceramic and Clay
800-999-2529
www.georgies.com
Complete line of candlemaking supplies

Glorybee
800-456-7923
www.glorybee.com
Beeswax candlemaking supplies

Knorr Beeswax
800-807-2337
www.knorrbeeswax.com
Beeswax rolling sheets and wicks

Mann Lake Ltd.
800-880-7694
www.mannlakeltd.com
Beeswax rolling sheets, molds, and wicks

Paplin Products
440-572-1086
www.paplin.com
Complete line of candlemaking supplies

Pourette Manufacturing
206-290-8214
www.pourette.com
Complete line of candlemaking supplies

Wicks & Wax
800-940-1232
www.wicksandwax.com
Beeswax candlemaking supplies

Yaley Enterprises
800-959-2539
www.yaley.com
Complete line of candlemaking supplies

Color and Scent Suppliers

Chemessence, Inc.
860-355-4108
www.chemessence.com

The Essential Oil Company
800-729-5912
www.essentialoil.com

French Color and Chemical Co.
800-762-9098

Lebermuth Company
800-648-1123
www.lebermuth.com

Pure Essential Inc.
519-488-1432
www.essential-oil.org

Pylam Products
800-645-6096
www.pylamdyes.com

Talisman Company
800-850-8101
www.madini.com
Wholesale Wax Suppliers

Frank B. Ross Company
732-669-0810
www.frankbross.com

The International Group
800-852-6537
www.igiwax.com

Just by Nature, Inc.
972-686-2929
www.justbynature.com

Koster Keunen
860-945-3333
www.kosterkeunen.com

Penreco
800-245-3952
www.penreco.com
Wholesalers of Versagel C Series Candle Gel

SouthWest Wax
866-799-2950
www.southwestwax.com

Mold-Making Supplies

North Valley Candle Molds
877-818-6653
www.moldman.com

Smooth-On Inc.
800-762-0744
www.smooth-on.com

Wax-Melting Systems

Melting and Filling Equipment, Inc.
866-740-6650
www.waxmelters.com

D. C. Cooper Company
800-536-9274
www.dccoopertanks.com

Maxant Industries
978-772-0576
www.maxantindustries.com

Waage Electric
908-245-9363
www.waage.com

For information about candles from the country's expert source, contact:

National Candle Association
202-393-2210
www.candles.org

READING LIST

The following list includes the books I have found most useful in my pursuit of candlemaking. While many of the books were written during the revival of the candlemaking craft in the 1970s, they still remain some of the best resources for a solid foundation in candlemaking techniques. Some books are now out of print, but I have been able to find all of them at my local library.

Brown, Donald S. *Candles.* 1979. (unpublished manuscript)

Carey, Mary. *Step by Step Candlemaking.* Racine, WI: Western Publishing Company, 1972.

Chaney, Charles and Skee, Stanley. *Plaster Mold and Model Making.* New York: Simon and Schuster, 1973.

Coggshall and Morse. *Beeswax, Production, Harvesting, Processing and Products.* Ithaca, NY: WICWAS Press, 1984.

Constable, David. *Candlemaking, Creative Designs and Techniques.* Great Britain: Search Press Ltd., 1992.

Creekmore, Betsey B. *Making Gifts from Oddments and Outdoor Materials.* New York: Hearthside Press, Inc., 1970.

Creekmore, Betsey B. *Traditional American Crafts.* New York: Hearthside Press Inc., 1968.

Dussek Campbell Inc., National Wax Division. *Candlemakers Guide,* vol. 1.04. Skokie, IL: Dussek Campbell Inc., 1995.

Gilbreath, Alice. *Candles for Beginners to Make.* New York: William Morris & Co., Inc., 1975.

Guy, Gary V. *Easy-to-Make Candles.* New York: Dover Publications, 1979.

Hart, Rhonda Massingham. *You Can Carve Fantastic Jack-O-Lanterns.* Pownal, VT: Storey Publishing, 1989.

Heller, Beatrice. *Introduction to Candlemaking: A Step by Step Guide.* Los Angeles: Nash Publishing, 1972.

Innes, Miranda. *The Book of Candles.* New York: Dorling Kindersley Inc., 1991.

Klenke, William W. *Candlemaking.* Peoria, IL: The Manual Arts Press, 1946.

Newman, Thelma. *Creative Candlemaking.* New York, NY: Crown Publishers, 1972.

Nussle, William. *Candle Crafting: From an Art to a Science.* South Brunswick, NJ and New York: A.S Barnes and Company, 1971.

Olsen, Don. *Candles That Earn.* Seattle, WA: Peanut Butter Publishing, 1990.

Pownall, Glen. *Lighting Crafts.* New Zealand: Seven Seas Publishing Pty. Ltd., 1974.

Rodale's Illustrated Encyclopedia of Herbs. Emmaus, PA: Rodale Press, 1987.

Root, A.I. *The ABC and XYZ of Bee Culture.* Medina, OH: The A.I. Root Co., 1954.

Shaw, Ray. *Candle Arts.* New York: William Morris & Co., Inc., 1973.

Strose, Suzanne. *Candlemaking.* New York: Sterling Publishing Co., Inc., 1968. Originally published as *Kerzen* (Munich: Don Bosco Verlag, 1967).

Walsh, William S. *Curiosities of Popular Culture.* New York: J.B. Lippincott Co., 1897.

Wels, Byron G. *Here Is Your Hobby.* New York: C.P. Putnam's Sons, 1977.

White, Elaine C. *Super Formulas: Arts and Crafts.* Starkville, MS: Valley Hills Press, 1993.

INDEX

Page numbers in *italic* indicate illustrations; those in **boldface** indicate charts

W

Water bath, 91
Wax
  amount needed, 43–45
  candleholders, 158–60,
    159, 160, 162–63, *163*
  on clothes, 66–67
  disposal of, 66
  history, 7
  melting, 57, 58–60, *59,* 99
  pouring, 59, 65, 79, *79,*
    80, *80*
  recipes, 40–42, 71–73, *72,*
    73
  recycled, 28–59
  types, 25–32 *(See also*
    specific types)

  whipped, 139, *139*
Wax infusion, 55
Wax shields, 157, *157*
Weights
  described, 61
  reusing, 113
White petrolatum, 36, **38**
Wick holders, 80
Wicks
  burning, 13–15, 23, *24,*
    24
  for candle gel, 83
  for cast shapes, 98
  centering in candles, 80
  defined, 13
  inserting in hardened
    candles, 21, *21,* 89, *89*

  inserting in molds, 88–89,
    88, 89
  making, 21–23
  priming, 19–20, *19, 20*
  selecting, 15, 71
  tabbing, 20, *20*
  trimming, 14
  types, *13,* 15–19, *16*
Work space
  cleaning up, 66–67, 75,
    85
  essentials for, 60
  newspaper in, 61
Wrapping, decorative,
  166–69, *167*

The Aromatherapy Companion, by Victoria H. Edwards.
The most comprehensive aromatherapy guide, filled with profiles
of essential oils and recipes for beauty, health, and well-being.
288 pages. Paper. ISBN-13: 978-1-58017-150-2.

Creating an Herbal Bodycare Business, by Sandy Maine.
An introduction to a new model: a business that is profitable
as well as socially and economically responsible.
160 pages. Paper. ISBN-13: 978-1-58017-094-9.

Creating Fairy Garden Fragrances, by Linda Gannon.
A beautifully illustrated, full-color book that explores
the world of fragrant blends made with essential oils and
dried flowers, herbs, and fruits.
64 pages. Hardcover with jacket. ISBN-13: 978-1-58017-076-5.

**The Essential Oils Book: Creating Personal Blends
for Mind & Body,** by Colleen K. Dodt.
A rich resource on the many uses of aromatherapy and its
applications in everyday life.
160 pages. Paper. ISBN-13: 978-0-88266-913-7.

Healing Tonics, by Jeanine Pollak.
Tasty, health-promoting recipes for drinks that can help
boost mental clarity, increase stamina, aid digestion,
support heart health, and more.
160 pages. Paper. ISBN-13: 978-1-58017-240-0.

The Herbal Home Remedy Book, by Joyce A. Wardwell.
A wealth of herbal healing wisdom, with advice on how to
collect and store herbs, make remedies, and stock a home
herbal medicine chest.
176 pages. Paper. ISBN-13: 978-1-58017-016-1.

The Herbal Home Spa: Naturally Refreshing Wraps,
Rubs, Lotions, Masks, Oils, and Scrubs, by Greta Breedlove.
A collection of easy-to-create personal care products that rival
potions found at exclusive spas and specialty shops.
208 pages. Paper. ISBN-13: 978-1-58017-005-5.

Herbal Teas, by Kathleen Brown.
A collection of blends to brew your own soothing,
invigorating, healthy, or just plain delicious teas.
160 pages. Paper. ISBN-13: 978-1-58017-099-4.

Keeping Life Simple, by Karen Levine.
Hundreds of practical tips and inspiring thoughts to
help you reduce clutter and focus on what really matters.
384 pages. Paper. ISBN-13: 978-1-58017-600-2.

Making Herbal Dream Pillows, by Jim Long.
Step-by-step instructions and lavish, full-color illustrations
that show how to create herbal dream blends and pillows.
64 pages. Hardcover with jacket. ISBN-13: 978-1-58017-075-8.

Making Natural Liquid Soaps, by Catherine Failor.
All-natural inexpensive hand soaps, shampoos, shower gels,
bubble baths, and more, using a double-boiler technique.
144 pages. Paper. ISBN-13: 978-1-58017-243-1.

Making Transparent Soap, by Catherine Failor.
Step-by-step directions to produce transparent soaps
that are mild, rich, and creamy.
144 pages. Paper. ISBN-13: 978-1-58017-244-8.

Melt & Mold Soap Crafting, by C. Kaila Westerman.
Colorful, eye-catching soaps, made in the microwave
without lye or other hazardous chemicals.
144 pages. Paper. ISBN-13: 978-1-58017-293-6.

Milk-Based Soaps, by Casey Makela.
Extensive coverage of the processes of making milk-based soaps,
long recognized for their gentleness and beautifying effects.
112 pages. Paper. ISBN-13: 978-0-88266-984-7.

Natural BabyCare, by Colleen K. Dodt.
Pure and soothing herbal recipes and techniques
to promote the health of mothers and babies.
160 pages. Paper. ISBN-13: 978-0-88266-953-3.

Natural Foot Care, by Stephanie Tourles.
A comprehensive handbook natural, homemade herbal treatments, massage techniques, and exercises for healthy feet.
192 pages. Paper. ISBN-13: 978-1-58017-054-3.

Naturally Healthy Skin, by Stephanie Tourles.
A total reference about caring for all types of skin, with
recipes, techniques, and practical advice.
208 pages. Paper. ISBN-13: 978-1-58017-130-4.

***The Natural Soap Book: Making Herbal and
Vegetable-Based Soaps,*** by Susan Miller Cavitch.
Basic recipes for soaps made without chemical additives and
synthetic ingredients, as well as ideas on scenting, coloring,
cutting, trimming, and wrapping soaps.
192 pages. Paper. ISBN-13: 978-0-88266-888-8.

Organic Body Care Recipes, by Stephanie Tourles.
Homemade, herbal formulas for glowing skin, hair,
and nails, plus a vibrant self.
384 pages. Paper. 978-1-58017-676-7.

Perfumes, Splashes & Colognes, by Nancy M. Booth.
Step-by-step, illustrated instructions for making personal
blends with herbs, essential oils, and fragrance oils.
176 pages. Paper. ISBN-13: 978-0-88266-985-4.

Simple Fountains, by Dorcas Adkins.
Simple, creative techniques for 20 projects, from a small tabletop
fountain to a dramatic outdoor spouting wall fountain.
160 pages. Paper. ISBN-13: 978-1-58017-506-7.

The Soapmaker's Companion, by Susan Miller Cavitch.
A resource for beginner and advanced soapmakers alike, from
mastering basic skills to creating soaps with a personal touch.
288 pages. Paper. ISBN-13: 978-0-88266-965-6.

Wabi Sabi: The Art of Everyday Life, by Diane Durston.
A giftbook that celebrates nature's simplicity and imperfection.
384 pages. Paper. ISBN-13: 978-1-58017-628-6.

These and other books from Storey Publishing are available
wherever quality books are sold or by calling 1-800-441-5700.
Visit us at *www.storey.com.*